CASE STUDIES IN
EDUCATION AND CULTURE

General Editors

GEORGE and LOUISE SPINDLER

Stanford University

GROWING UP IN TWO WORLDS

Education and Transition among the Sisala of Northern Ghana

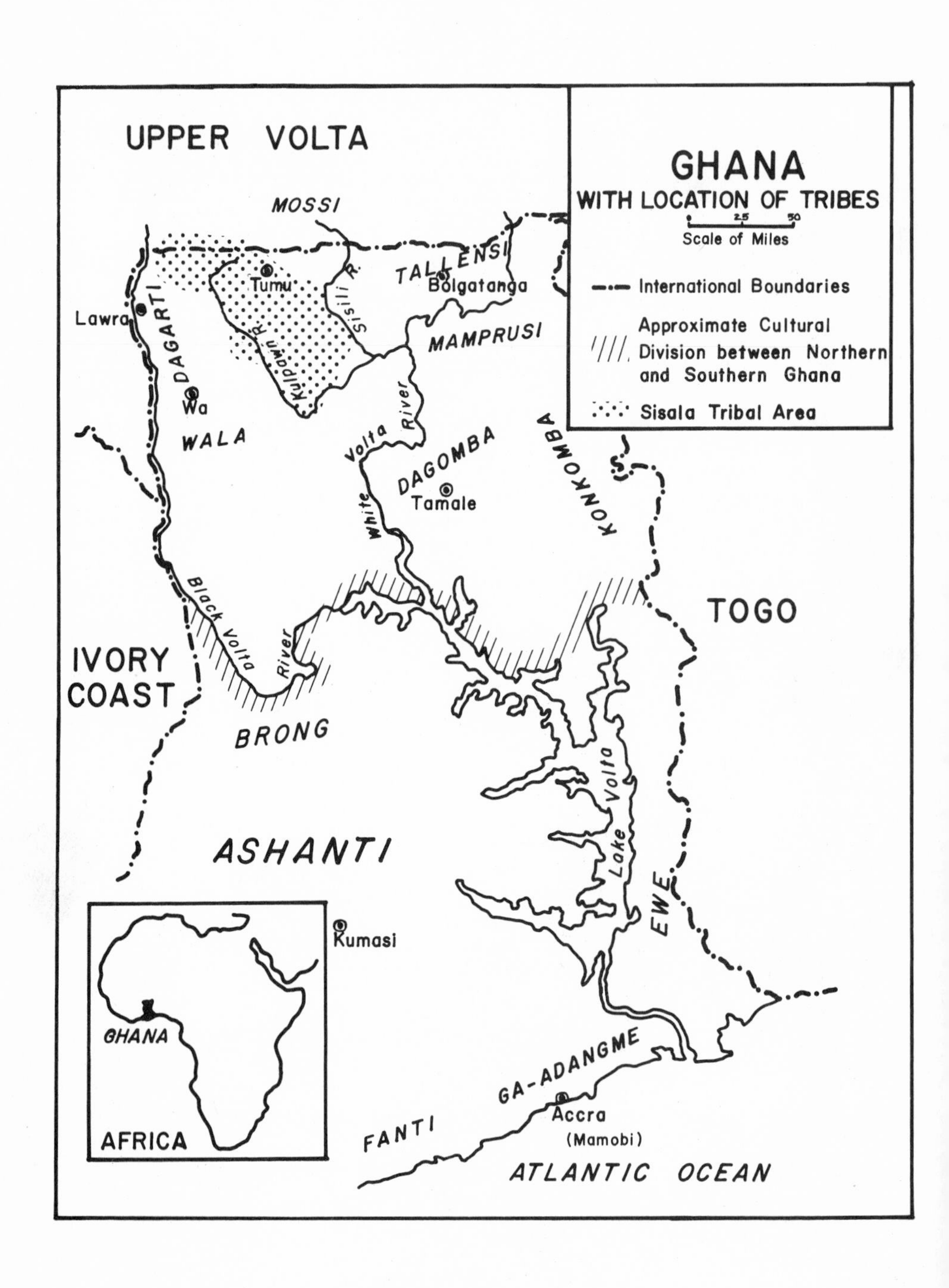
GHANA
WITH LOCATION OF TRIBES
25
50
Scale of Miles
International Boundaries
Approximate Cultural Division between Northern and Southern Ghana
Sisala Tribal Area
UPPER VOLTA
MOSSI
TALLENSI
Bolgatanga
Tumu
Lawra
DAGARTI
Sisili R.
Kulpawn R.
MAMPRUSI
Wa
WALA
White Volta River
DAGOMBA
Tamale
KONKOMBA
Black Volta River
TOGO
IVORY COAST
BRONG
Lake Volta
ASHANTI
EWE
Kumasi
GHANA
AFRICA
GA-ADANGME
Accra
(Mamobi)
FANTI
ATLANTIC OCEAN

GROWING UP IN TWO WORLDS

Education and Transition among the Sisala of Northern Ghana

BRUCE T. GRINDAL
Middlebury College

HOLT, RINEHART AND WINSTON, INC.
New York · Chicago · San Francisco · Atlanta
Dallas · Montreal · Toronto · London · Sydney

Library of Congress Catalog Card Number: 70-168982
ISBN: 0-03-086549-2
Printed in the United States of America
2 3 4 5 6 059 9 8 7 6 5 4 3 2 1

Foreword

About the Series

This series of case studies in education and culture is designed to bring to students in professional education and in the social sciences the results of direct observation and participation in the educational process in a variety of cultural settings. Individual studies include some devoted to single classrooms, others focus on single schools, some on large communities and their schools; still others report on indigenous cultural transmission where there are no schools at all in the Western sense. Every attempt is made to move beyond the formalistic treatments of educational process to the interaction between the people engaged in educative events, their thinking and feeling, and the content of the educational process in which they are engaged. Each study is basically descriptive in character but since all of them are about education they are also problem oriented. Interpretive generalizations are produced inductively. Some are stated explicitly by the authors of the studies. Others are generated in the reader's mind as hypotheses about education and its environmental relationships.

The cross-cultural emphasis of the series is particularly significant. Education is a cultural process. Each new member of a society or a group must learn to act appropriately as a member and contribute to its maintenance and, occasionally, to its improvement. Education, in every cultural setting, is an instrument for survival. It is also an instrument for adaptation and change. To understand education we must study it as it is—imbedded in the culture of which it is an integral part and which it serves.

When education is studied this way, the generalizations about the relationship between schools and communities, educational and social systems, education and cultural setting that are current in modern educational discussions become meaningful. This series is, therefore, intended for use in courses in comparative and overseas education, social foundations and the sociology of education, international educational development, culture and personality, social psychology, cultural dynamics and cultural transmission, comparative sociology—wherever the interdependency of education and culture, and education and society, is particularly relevant.

We hope these studies will be useful as resources for comparative analyses, and for stimulating thinking and discussion about education that is not confined by one's own cultural experience. Without this exercise of a comparative, transcultural perspective it seems unlikely that we can acquire a clear view of our own educational experience or view education in other cultural settings without ethnocentric bias.

About the Author

Bruce T. Grindal was born near Chicago in 1940. He completed his undergraduate degree at Northwestern University in 1963 and his doctoral degree in anthropology at Indiana University in 1969. On a grant from the Foreign Area Fellowship Program he spent nineteen months in Ghana living and conducting research among the Sisala people. He is currently an assistant professor in the Department of Sociology-Anthropology at Middlebury College in Vermont.

About the Book

This is a study of traditional and modern educational processes at work within a tribal society, the Sisala of Northern Ghana. These processes are not treated as abstractions. The individual is educated by his traditional relationships with family and kin, and also by his experience with modern schools and with migration. Traditional education in Sisala society is a gradual process. Children are born into large extended family households where they are viewed as belonging to everyone and not just to their parents. Stress is placed upon compliance and respect, unity and cooperation. By age six a child begins to participate in work tasks of household and farm. A strong identification with family and kin is developed.

With the background on the traditional educational experiences established, the author discusses the modern educational experience. Together with the effects of recent British rule and contact with the urban centers of southern Ghana, modern education has contributed to changes in child training and to a breakdown of traditional values governing property, authority, and the supernatural. Education is seen by the people as the path to achievement, self-improvement, and autonomy, but they also see that it is destructive of the continuity between generations and the maintenance of the established culture. Much is lost for something gained.

Everywhere in the world where traditional systems of culture and the educational processes upholding them are confronted with modernization, the same dilemmas and potential consequences are faced. The Sisala model as described in this case study is applicable to a wide variety of specific situations elsewhere in the world.

George and Louise Spindler
General Editors

Acknowledgments

My field research among the Sisala people was undertaken over a nineteen-month period from September 1966 through March 1968 on a grant from the Foreign Area Fellowship Program.

The first three months were spent in Accra, Ghana, engaging in preparatory ethnographic and historical research at the University of Ghana and Ghana National Archives, and pursuing independent linguistic research with Sisala informants. Also, prior to arriving in Ghana I spent one week at the Summer Institute of Linguistics in Redhill, England, consulting with Ron Rowland about his research into the Sisala language.

From December 1966 to March 1967, and again from June 1967 to March 1968, I worked among the Sisala of the Tumu District in northern Ghana, residing in the town of Tumu, capital of the district. My research was about evenly divided between Tumu and a nearby village, Sorbelle. From March to June of 1967, I returned to Accra where I conducted a study of Sisala migrants living in the northern tribal migrant settlement of Mamobi.

My research would not have been possible without the cooperation and interest of the Sisala and the people of Tumu, Sorbelle, and Mamobi. In addition, I wish to thank the Foreign Area Fellowship Program for supporting my research and the write-up of my dissertation. I am indebted to Ron Rowland, Ivor Wilks, Jeffery Holden, and Roy Sieber for their aid and advice concerning the substantive areas of my research. Special thanks go to Professor Alan P. Merriam for his guidance, encouragement, and critical appraisal of my work, and to Professors David Bidney, Richard Antoun, and Roy Sieber for the reading of my dissertation. Lastly, I am indebted to my parents, and to my wife, Mary, whose warmth and facility in establishing personal relationships provided the necessary balance to my scholarly research.

B. T. G.

Pronunciation Guide

Throughout the book certain terms and statements are referred to in the Sisala language. In most instances the Sisala usage is given in parentheses immediately following the English equivalent. However, in cases where the Sisala term is cited frequently, the English translation does not appear and reference is made in the glossary.

The pronunciation of Sisala consonants is basically similar to their English equivalents. There are two exceptions, however; these are the labio-velar double stops *kp* and *gb* which do not occur in English but which may be reproduced by pronouncing both consonant sounds simultaneously. The spelling orthography for vowels follows the Americanist phonetic usage. However, in order to avoid typesetting difficulties, no distinction has been made between open and close vowels. The vowel sounds are indicated as follows:

i, like the *i* in bit

e, like the *e* in net

a, like the *a* in father

u, like the *oo* in boot

o, like the *o* in motive

Contents

Introduction

THIS STUDY is an investigation of the nature of education and its relationship to the social development of the individual and the process of sociocultural change among the Sisala of northern Ghana. By "education" I refer here to two distinct, though interrelated, processes of cultural transmission. On one hand, there is the traditional educational experience as manifested in the child-training practices and life cycle of the Sisala. In this context of family, village, and tribe, the individual learns the necessary values, knowledge, techniques, and other prerequisites for adult life in the tribal setting. By contrast, there is what I term the modern educational experience; this would include any experience which occurs outside of, or is not related to, the traditional cultural setting and network of social relationships. The young man who migrates outside the tribe in search of wage employment or the schoolboy who learns from a British patterned curriculum, both encounter experiences which are different from, and oftentimes in conflict with, those encountered in the traditional setting. To what degree these experiences create conflicts between traditionally held and newly acquired values and in turn affect the individual's relationships with others in the society is a main concern of this investigation.

In large part this study reflects a growing need to relate the traditional approaches of anthropology to the contemporary social realities of developing societies. In the past, anthropologists have conducted their work almost solely within the context of small, homogeneous, nonliterate societies. These societies tend to be viewed as stable and continuous over time, and education is likewise seen as part of this continuous process wherein the child grows up to assume his father's position and to maintain and perpetuate actively the society of which he is a product. However, in recent times, with the struggle for nationalism and independence, the arbitrarily defined colonial territories of European nations have become functionally integrated sociopolitical units with a growing set of national traditions. In the African nation-states the phenomena of modern education, migration, and the mass media have resulted in the breakdown of cultural communication barriers and the creation of a pantribal or national sociocultural base. While the traditional or tribal society remains a meaningful unit of analysis, it does not constitute the sole perspective. Thus, the contemporary situation demands that we examine the larger sociocultural context within which the tribal society exists and the individual interacts.

In this modern setting the individual grows up to experience two sociocultural worlds: the traditional world of village and tribe and the modern world as defined by the larger socioeconomic and sociopolitical structure of the nation-state. The traditional model of the mutually reinforcing relationship between the educational experience and the continuity of the tribal society is no longer sufficient since the learning experiences of early childhood provide but a partial basis for the individual's adult identity. Instead, the individual is a product of two sociocultural worlds from which he must choose among their differing and often conflicting perspectives.

In terms of the model underlying this presentation the individual is viewed as a mediator in the change or acculturative process. By maintaining relationships in the modern sphere of the society (for example, in his role as migrant or schoolboy), he becomes acculturated; by maintaining relationships in the traditional sphere of the society, he becomes an agent of acculturation affecting change in his interaction with the more traditionally oriented members of his family, village, and tribe. Thus, as changes in interaction patterns and social relationships become cumulative and as these changes in turn affect patterns of child rearing, the larger institutional structure and customary code of the traditional society is affected.

The Sisala people clearly suit the purposes of this study. In comparison with the other tribes of Ghana the Sisala have not been subjected to intensive modernizing influences. The traditional structure of authority and subsistence pursuits of the people remain essentially intact, as well as the

A view of Tumu.

rule of patrilineal descent which serves as the primary idiom of the social structure. Nonetheless, the modern society has made inroads with the establishment of schools, local government councils, and intertribal commerce. Graded roads cut through the Sisala area and motorized vehicles carry people and farm produce to the surrounding trading centers in Bolgatanga, Wa, and the larger cities of southern Ghana. Today the Sisala people are part of the modern nation-state of Ghana. The tribal area, now included within the Tumu Administrative District, boasts of its own local government and representative in the Ghanaian national Parliament.

This juxtaposition of the old and the new is well illustrated in the district capital of Tumu where I resided during my field research. Tumu may best be seen as both a traditional village and a modern town. As a village it consists of nine lineage settlements which are related through patrilineal descent to form a single clan. The head of the clan is chief, and along with the elders of the other lineage settlements, he is responsible for the conduct of traditional village affairs. Superimposed upon this village organization is Tumu the modern town. Approximately one-half of its near 3000 population is made up of strangers, including traders and artisans from other tribes, government officials and civil servants, and Sisala from other villages. The town has three primary schools, two upper primary or middle schools,[1] a teacher training college, two mosques, an electrically lit beer bar, a motorized transport center, government offices, a health center, living quarters for government employees and teachers, and a large "zongo" or stranger's section. Located at the crossroads of the main transportation routes, Tumu is the center of diffusion from which changes spread throughout the tribal area.

In order to gain additional perspective and to provide a continuum along which the change process could be explained, two additional areas of research were selected: the village of Sorbelle and the town of Mamobi, a tribal migrant settlement in Accra, the capital city of Ghana. The village of Sorbelle is located four-and-one-half miles west of Tumu, and except for the presence of a two-room schoolhouse, it is typical of the less acculturated Sisala villages. This area was chosen to provide perspective on the traditional society and the nature of the traditional educational experience. The study of Mamobi town, on the other hand, was aimed at gaining an understanding of the Sisala's migratory experience in terms of the reactions and adaptations to life in a large city.

The data used in this study are essentially behavioral, derived from interviews, informal conversations, and observations of the daily cultural routine. Special emphasis was placed upon life history materials, examining

[1] In Ghana, the primary school includes the first through sixth grades (or forms) and the middle school, the seventh through tenth grades. Following graduation from middle school, the student may qualify for secondary education which is generally a four-year course. The teacher training college is one form of secondary education. (The other forms are regular secondary school and technical or vocational school.) Beyond this, the next step is university education.

the varieties of the individual's experiences, his reactions to these experiences, and his particular adjustment in the society. Child-training interviews, based upon a questionnaire by Landy (1959), were administered to both men and women; these provided information relevant not only to an understanding of traditional education as represented in the villages but also to changes in the individual's social environment resulting from acculturation. Lastly emphasis was given to an examination of the modern educational process within the schoolroom setting.

In addition, projective essays and tests were administered to schoolchildren. These helped to provide a quantitative perspective, and they served to uncover questions and provide insights which were subsequently cross-checked by interviews and other ethnographic observations. In the latter section of Chapter 5, major emphasis is given to data derived from a projective autobiographical essay entitled, "My Autobiography from Now to the Year 2000." This device was used elsewhere by Allport and Gillespie (1955) in a crossnational study of youth's outlook on the future. In the case of my research it was administered to students in the middle schools and the teacher training college of Tumu for the purpose of gaining insight into the students' attitude toward the educational process and into their perception of themselves both as students and as future successful adults.

1/The Sisala people: their history and society

The Sisala people are situated primarily in northwestern Ghana, but include a small population in Upper Volta. They are bound on the west and south by the Kulpawn River and on the east by the Sisili River. The Sisala language, Isalang, belongs to the Grusi subfamily of the Voltaic language family; as of 1960, 59,000 Isalang speakers resided in Ghana (Ghana Census Office 1964).

As Voltaic speakers they share linguistic and cultural affinities with most of the other tribes of northern Ghana, including the Dagomba, Mamprusi, Tallensi, Wala, Konkomba, and Dagarti. This area in which these groups live, north of the Black Volta River, is Guinea savannah woodland, consisting of wide stretches of grassland interspersed with trees and scrub bush. Rainfall is low with pronounced seasonal variations resulting in a long and intensely hot dry season from November to April. To the south of the Black Volta River are situated the Kwa-speaking peoples of the rain forest, the larger tribes consisting of the Ewe, Ga-Adangme, and Akan-speaking Ashanti, Fanti, and Brong.

This cultural and ecological division of Ghana between the Voltaic-speaking North and the Kwa-speaking South is paralleled by differences in the modern historical development of these two areas. Prior to its independence in 1957 Ghana (at that time known as the Gold Coast) was a British colony. During colonial times the Gold Coast was divided into three administrative regions: the Gold Coast Colony, the Ashanti Confederacy, and the Northern Territories. Referred to by the Sisala as "the South," the first two administrative regions have had a relatively long tradition of British rule, and its tribes are more acculturated than those of the North. The Northern Territories were regarded as a cultural backwash by the British, and little attempt was made to develop its commercial potential or to introduce educational facilities; indeed, until World War II the major aim of colonial policy in the North was the simple maintenance of law and order. Lack of roads and transport facilities have also helped to widen the gap between the isolated northern tribes and the rapidly modernizing South.

This isolation was particularly acute among the Sisala. The British first established their presence in the Sisala area in 1906 with the construction of a government station in the town of Tumu. British colonial policy during these early years was inconsistent and ineffective. Most of the British

Dry season Guinea savannah landscape.

colonial officers or district commissioners were army officers, living without their wives in a rough and relatively inaccessible region. In their diaries many officers expressed a distaste for their work and skepticism about its effectiveness. One of the reasons for this ineffectiveness was the short terms of office; between 1906 and 1920, nineteen district commissioners were stationed in Tumu, with a consequent dislocation of effective planning. Attempts were made to institute sanitation, road work, trade and firearms tax, and a local court, but none proved successful. All the colonial officers except one showed an indifference to Sisala custom. In 1920 the Tumu station was closed, the rationale being that law and order prevailed and that no further need for the British presence was evident. From 1920 to 1946 the Tumu District was merged with the Lawra District in the Dagarti tribal area with the administrative headquarters in the town of Lawra. This led to further dislocation of planning, and many of the roads in the area fell into complete disrepair, thereby restricting even further the people's contact with the outside world.

In reaction to the growing nationalistic fervor in the Gold Coast and in anticipation of Ghana's eventual independence, the British reluctantly reopened the government station in Tumu in 1946. With the establishment of educational facilities and other government services the first serious attempt was made to prepare the Sisala for self-government and entry into the modern world. The evolution of Tumu from a virtually traditional village to a modern town thus represents a recent historical development.

However, as one moves away from Tumu along the graded roads and then along the narrow footpaths which wind through the countryside, the modernizing influences of recent times become less intense. Small but highly compact villages dot the sparsely populated savannah landscape. Passing through a village, one may occasionally see situated along the road a mud brick bungalow with a corrugated aluminum roof built perhaps by one of the more wealthy or acculturated members of the town. The far greater percentage of the people, however, live in large mud-walled compounds located upon their traditional ancestral sites, usually under the shade of the huge and almost ageless baobaob trees. These more or less circular compounds are made up of rectangular brick dwellings which are linked together so as to present a sturdy wall to the outside world.

Around the compound may be found small gardens in which women grow tomatoes, onions, okra, red peppers, and other minor ingredients used in their cooking. At some distance from the village are located the main farms where the dietary staples of the people are grown, including primarily millet and guinea corn, but also maize, yams, peanuts, rice, and beans. While an occasional farmer may hire out a tractor to break the soil, the majority employ the traditional short-handled hoe and digging stick. Large livestock—cattle, sheep, and goats—are also kept but are of subsidiary dietary importance and are seldom sold for money; instead they serve as symbols of family prestige and are reserved mainly for customary economic transactions and for sacrifice to family and village shrines.

Thus, for the majority of the people the traditional economic and social structure of the society continues to function, and notwithstanding the presence of modern influences, it will probably continue to function for an indefinite future. Therefore, I should now like briefly to examine the traditional society both as an introduction to the discussion of the traditional educational experience and as a baseline for the evaluation of recent sociocultural change.

Sisala social organization is based upon the principle of patrilineal descent which serves to define interpersonal and intergroup relationships in the society. As among other African peoples, this descent system is segmental and hierarchical; thus any Sisala man can trace his affiliation beginning with his immediate family and continuing on through the male line to successively larger and more inclusive groupings or segments. The smaller groupings are called lineages and clan sections while the largest is the patriclan (*-viara*). All these groupings maintain the belief of common genetic descent from a founding ancestor. However, in the case of the patriclan these ties are often so remote that the ancestral connections among clan members take on legendary proportions. Also while the lineage and clan sections have definite economic, jural, and religious functions within the village context, the functions of the patriclan are more variable and less definite. In cases where the clan is highly localized in terms of a particular area of land (*tintein*), the sense of allegiance is often quite strong, and formerly during times of warfare its members would unite against a common enemy. For the most part, however, the membership of a given clan is so widely scattered over the Sisala area that the feeling of allegiance is purely nominal.

In addition to the rule of patrilineal descent, there exists a strong sense of village affiliation which stems in large part from a history of warfare and slave raiding which occurred prior to British contact during the nineteenth century. In the early 1860s, during the time of Ashanti expansion into northern Ghana, the Dagomba kingdom employed a group of Songhai-speaking Zabirama horsemen as traders and mercenaries to raid for slaves which were given as tribute to the Ashanti. By the late 1880s the Zabirama had become independent of their Dagomba masters and established their rule over a large part of northwest Ghana with their central power base within the Sisala area. Their rule, however, was short-lived, for they were defeated by the British in 1897. Nevertheless, this brief history of warfare caused considerable disruption and movement of populations; patriclans which at one time were unified in a particular locale were forced to split up and migrate. Sections of these clans thus came to settle in villages far from their ancestral homelands, and the alliance of the migrating clan section and its host village was most likely motivated out of the need for mutual defense. In contrast then to many of the neighboring tribes who have not had a history of warfare and whose settlements consist of dispersed homesteads, the Sisala live in compact villages numbering from 200 to 3000 persons and usually consisting of a plurality of clan sections, each claiming a different origin.

The compound or domestic household unit is the large patrilocal extended family (*janwuo*) consisting of the families of procreation of at least two siblings or patrilineally related cousins of the senior generation and depending upon the particular stage of the developmental cycle, the families of procreation of the male members of the descending generation. The *janwuo* averages over fifty members (Ghana Census Office 1964) and is further broken down into the nuclear and polygynous family households of the respective adult male members. A woman and her small children occupy a separate dwelling apart from that of the husband in the case of polygynous marriages; otherwise the nuclear family unit is usually situated in a single house. While female children reside with their mothers until marriage, boys six and older live with a senior male member in the *janwuo*.

Sisala marital unions are preferentially polygynous with sororal unions preferred. The rationale is that sisters do not quarrel as do women who are strangers to each other. Since residence is patrilocal, it is the woman who upon marriage must leave her family to join that of her husband and his people. Marriages are arranged between the extended families of the prospective husband and wife and involve the payment of a bride price (*jaraang*), usually a cow, by the groom's family to the wife's kin. This payment cements the conjugal relationship and gives the husband and his family jural rights in the offspring of the wife.

The extended family is the basic economically corporate, property-holding unit. The head of the *janwuo*, the *diatina* or "house owner," controls the use and distribution of large livestock and food produce from the family farm. Small livestock, including fowls and in some cases goats, and produce from small private plots may be owned by individual adult members of the *janwuo*. The *diatina* is automatically the eldest male member of the extended

An overview of the janwuo.

family; upon his death the office passes to the next eldest member of the senior generation and eventually to the oldest male of the junior generation.

Patrilineally related extended families combine to form a minor lineage settlement (*jechiking*). The component extended families are in very close physical proximity to one another, separated only by narrow passageways. The reason for this compactness, according to the Sisala, stems from the need for common defense and for protection against wild animals and witches (*hila*). The functions of the minor lineage settlements are jural and religious with disputes and quarrels among its members settled by the eldest house owner of the representative extended families. Sacrifices to certain shrines (*vene*) are attended by all members of the minor lineage. Unlike many of the neighboring tribes which live in small dispersed homesteads, the minor lineage settlement as a physical structure has a considerable degree of permanence, with subsequent generations living in the same houses as their forefathers.

One or more minor lineage settlements combine to form a clan section or maximal lineage within the village. An individual refers to members of his clan section, apart from those of his own minor lineage, as *nyinia* or "father's people" since all of its members may be traced to a single common ancestor who first settled in the village. As with the minor lineage settlement, the functions of the clan section are jural and ritual. Informal headmanship is based on age and thus rotates over time among the component extended families. Each clan section, regardless of size, possesses a shrine which is similar in name to the shrines of clan sections in other villages belonging to the same clan. Unless members of the same clan live in close proximity to one another, the similarity among their shrines is purely nominal, and the members of each clan section perform their sacrifices separately from their distant clan brothers.

A village usually consists of two large clan sections and a number of smaller ones; the smaller sections relate or ally themselves to one of the larger sections either through matrilineal or fictional kinship ties. Although the smaller sections do not sacrifice or have ritual obligations with the members of the larger section, they sit in council with them, form alliances in matters of intravillage dispute, and share their farm land (*baga*).

British colonial rule over the past half century has modified the political structure of Sisala society by the introduction of the institution of village chieftaincy as well as by the establishment of the town of Tumu as the seat of the paramount chief of all the Sisala. Prior to this time the Sisala did not have chiefs, and village authority was represented solely in the office of the *jangtina* or "village owner." Succession to this office, with some exceptions, was—and still is—restricted to that clan section believed to have first settled the area where the village is situated. The power of the *jangtina* is essentially ritual; he performs sacrifices and administers oaths to the village shrine, which is also the shrine of the clan section of the original founders. All members of the village, whatever their origin and descent affiliations, give respect to the *jangtina* as "first among equals" and to the efficacy of the village shrine. Except for the ritual and jural powers emanating from the village owner's relationship to his shrine, the real locus of authority resides in the economic and property rights of the headmen of the respective extended families.

Sisala beliefs in the supernatural closely parallel the nature of village social organization. Basic to the religious system is a belief in a male high god (*wia*), who is symbolically associated with the sky and the sun, and his "wife," the "Earth" (*tintein*). God is closely related to the notion of fate or "what god brings down" (*wia ne longe*). During sacrifices "God and his wife Earth" (*wia ari haala tintein*) are acknowledged, but beyond this no cult of worship exists, and these gods are not viewed as having direct association with the everyday affairs of man. Lesser spiritual entities are termed *vesing*, and they include the village and clan section spiritual shrines (*vene*); the ancestors (*lele*), whose shrines are generally located either within the extended family or minor lineage settlement; personal spirits (*tome*) and their shrines; medicines (*dalusun*); and a variety of nature spirits associated with trees (*tia*), the river (*fuo*), and the farm (*baga*).

2/The traditional educational experience

BIRTH IN THE CULTURAL CONTEXT

To the Sisala the birth of a child is an event of great joy. To the mother the first born child symbolizes her becoming a woman, and each subsequent child further cements the marital bond between her and her husband and increases her stature in the eyes of her husband's family. The father of many children commands respect since the potential labor of his offspring will eventually contribute to his wealth and position in society. For the society at large the birth of children is viewed as vital to the continuity of the extended family, and this is pointed up by the common Sisala saying, "Your child is your brother's child, and your brother's child is your child." Not only are children seen as potential contributors to the sustenance and perpetuation of the *janwuo* (patrilocal extended family), but birth itself is attributed to the favorable disposition of God and the ancestors. This importance attributed to birth is reflected in the elaboration of customs and ceremonies surrounding it.

Conception and pregnancy are regarded as natural processes in the life of a woman and thus cause for little concern. The pregnant woman is expected to accept "what God has brought down" and to look forward in happy anticipation to the birth of her child. Little change is introduced into her daily routine during pregnancy, and she continues to perform her regular duties until the seventh month when she assumes lighter tasks.

Beneath this facade of unconcern, however, lies the awareness of the dangers of pregnancy and childbirth. Childbirth is seen as a fearful occasion, and the phrase "giving birth in blood" is frequently used to describe the event. The high rate of mother mortality in childbirth serves only to increase the level of anxiety as the time for birth approaches. While men refuse to talk about matters of pregnancy, the expectant mother often consults a *hachikuoro,* an older woman who is specialized in the traditional art of prenatal medicine and midwifery. The midwife examines the woman to determine "how the conception lies" and prescribes massages and herbal medicines to ease delivery and prevent hemorrhaging.

A woman's first pregnancy is kept secret, for if attention is drawn to the fact, it is believed that she will miscarry. Even the expectant mother is not supposed to be aware of her condition until the ceremony termed *pose* or "pouring [water]" is performed during the fifth or sixth month of pregnancy. When the time arrives, the husband contacts one of his sisters who lives in another village and instructs her to perform the ceremony. In the night when all is quiet, the sister arrives in her brother's *janwuo* and enters the room where he and his wife are sleeping. Waking the brother quietly, she bids him to move aside. She then empties a calabash of water over the expectant mother, saying as she does, "Take my oil and give me my [dawa dawa] seed" (*la mi nu ang tia mi tua*). After this ceremony members of the husband's *janwuo* are free to call attention to the mother's condition and joke with her. Often they call her a thief for having taken one of their children.

A second ceremony must be performed for the protection and well-being of the unborn child. Called *wencheming* or "meeting on the road," it involves both the husband's and wife's families. Immediately after the ceremony of "pouring water," a representative of the husband's *janwuo* is sent to the wife's village to inform her parents that their daughter is pregnant. Both the husband's and wife's families then prepare a variety of different foods, and on the date arranged by the wife's parents, women from both families carrying the food meet at a halfway point between the two villages. A small boy from the husband's village wrestles with a boy of similar age from the wife's village and the former family always wins the contest. When he throws his opponent to the ground, he says, "Give me my child" (*tiam bi*). In the improbable event that the boy from the wife's village accidentally wins the match, it is believed that the newly born baby will die, since it would mean that the "wife had conquered the husband." After this the food is exchanged and both parties return to their respective villages.

These customs function to establish the rights of the husband and his family to the offspring of the expectant mother. In the *pose* ceremony the father's sister or "female father" (*nyilma*) of the expected baby acts as a representative of her brother's family when she symbolically demands that the expectant mother give over her "seed." Likewise, the *wencheming* ceremony represents the symbolic victory of the husband's people.

The early years of marriage are generally regarded by the people as unstable. The wife often returns to her own natal family and refuses to rejoin her husband. For this reason the husband's *janwuo* is often reluctant to give the bride wealth to the wife's family until the wife is firmly established in the husband's *janwuo*—that is, until she has given birth to many children. The *pose* and *wencheming* ceremonies point out the greater value attached to the woman's role as mother and childbearer than to her role as wife and consort.

Although the *pose* and *wencheming* ceremonies have been performed to insure the protection of the husband's family, the possibility of death is present in the minds of all. When labor begins, the expectant mother retires to her own room to be joined by a midwife and two older women who assist in the delivery. She delivers in a squatting position, with the two assistants holding her up and the midwife performing the actual delivery. As soon as the child is born, one of the women assisting the midwife utters a cry, announcing the arrival of the child.

Although much of the tension is relieved following the birth, the welfare of the infant remains a matter of great concern. It is believed that from birth to the age of three days in the case of a boy and four days in the case of a girl, the new born baby is not yet a *nibiing* or "child among people." As such it is in constant danger of death from sickness or malevolent supernatural forces. During this period the infant remains indoors and is in the constant presence of the mother. Other than the husband only the midwife and her assistants may be present at this time. The Sisala believe that evil people or witches (*hila* and *nyisi*) may be jealous of the baby and attempt to steal its soul (*dima*).

Both the father's and mother's families contribute to the protection of the child. When a child is born, the *diatina* (head of the father's family) places a shrine at the infant's feet. This shrine consists of a pot which is kept with the ancestral shrine within the *janwuo*. Since it is therefore portable, it may be removed from the ancestral shrine house whenever a new child is born. When the shrine is placed at the baby's feet, the *diatina* pours sacrificial water over it, saying, "There is a child born. You (ancestors) are the grandfather and grandmother of the newborn baby and you must take care of it whenever the mother and father go." Thus, the shrine will guard the baby and protect him from anybody wishing to harm him.

Soon after the birth of the child the husband sets out for the wife's village, taking with him a white cock or hen according to the sex of the baby. He must perform his mission in complete silence and may neither look behind him nor speak to anyone on the road. He walks straight to his wife's parents' compound and remains standing until the wife's father comes to take the fowl. In return he is given a medicine called *kantong luri* or "fairy medicine." He returns by the same route along which he came and gives the medicine to the *diatina* who in turn places it at the child's head. This custom signifies that while the wife's people recognize the husband's rights to the newborn child, they are also concerned with his welfare. As the Sisala say, "A man never forgets his daughter's child" (*tolobie*).

If the child is stillborn or if he dies during the period of seclusion, his body is disposed of in a manner similar to the disposal of the afterbirth, for it is not until three days for a boy or four days for a girl that the child is regarded as human (*nibie*) and deserving of a proper human burial. The child's body is placed in a pot and unceremoniously buried outside near the wall of the *janwuo*. The cause of death may be attributed either to weakness or infirmity of the child or to the violation of ancestral custom and taboo, such as previous unconfessed adulterous union on the part of the mother.

If the child survives the period of seclusion, the "outdooring" or "ceremony of the rooftop" is performed. Great suspense is involved in this ceremony, and it is carried out in great secrecy during the night of the third or fourth day of the child's seclusion. If a person coughs or a dog barks, it is believed that the child will die. In silence, then, the mother of the infant climbs to the roof of her house, followed by a younger sister of the father's mother. Another woman from the father's mother's village stands below holding the infant. The latter addresses the father's mother's sister on the roof, saying, "The infant wants to go on the roof," and hands up the child. The woman on the roof then says, "The child wants to enter the room," and hands the child down. This process is repeated three or four times according to the sex of the child. After this ceremony the mother and child are allowed to move freely in the compound.

The "ceremony of the rooftop" symbolically represents the incorporation of the child into the physical and social space of the living. Prior to the ceremony the baby was secluded within the confines of the mother's room, protected from the possible malevolence of the outer world by shrines and medicines (*dalusun*). Although the Sisala were either unable or unwilling to explain the precise significance of this ceremony, one elder man remarked that it brought to mind the proverb, "A worm comes out into the sun to die" (*wering si li wiheye n lia ding su ne*). He continued, "This proverb [*namaka*] means that all men are born to suffer and eventually die. When a baby is born, it cries because it must suffer. In the same way, when a child is a few days old, it must go outside, for it cannot remain forever in its mother's room." In symbolic terms, then, the "outdooring" may be likened to a second birth wherein the baby moves from the seclusion and protection of the mother's room to the unprotected and often harsh reality of the outer world.

Although the Sisala believe that the birth of a child is determined by fate or "by God," the cause of birth is also seen in terms of the lesser deities and the ancestors. Immediately after the birth the father or some other male member of the father's family will consult a diviner (*vuruga*) to determine the name which the child should be given. It is believed that in most cases the child is reincarnated, and the name given to him is determined by the particular spiritual entity responsible for the reincarnation. If the child is reincarnated by an ancestor, he is given the name of that particular ancestor. An infant may also be reincarnated by the spiritual entities related to shrines within the village or the extended family. The following are common Sisala names related to spiritual entities:

1. Dima (male) and Hadima (female). Related to the *dima* or "soul shrine."
2. Batong and Hatong. Related to the *tong* or *tome* or "hunting spirit."
3. Luri and Haluri. Related to the *luri* or "xylophone spirit."

After the father or elder man has consulted the diviner, he is enjoined from divulging the name until the naming ceremony. If anyone in the compound chances to say the child's name during this time, and if the child hears it, it is believed that he will die. When the ancestor or spirit reincarnates in a child, he is believed to be thirsty and will remain so until he is sacrificed to and "given water" at the naming ceremony. Thus, if the ancestor or spirit reincarnated in the child hears its name spoken, he will think his name is being "spoiled," and he will become angry and "go back" because it feels that the people do not respect it.

A diviner (vuruga) *is consulted to determine the name of a newly born child.*

The naming ceremony takes place very early in the morning in the room in which the ancestral shrine is kept. The night before the *diatina* of the father's *janwuo* notifies the people of his clan section, saying that he is going to "give water" to the ancestors in their house and that they should not go anywhere until he has done so. When everyone has gathered, the *diatina* proceeds to offer water and sacrifice fowls while calling the ancestors, God, Earth, and the shrines and medicines of the *janwuo.* A sheep is then slaughtered and the *diatina* says, "This is for the visitor. This is his food." The baby is then brought in, and the *diatina* holds it in his arms and calls out the name for the first time. The name is called three times for a boy and four times for a girl. The diatina then says, "You have come back to us. You will have to bring us peace. Let us have good yield. Keep the house well and don't let any trouble come to us. You have to sleep soundly and let your mother do any kind of work she has to do in the house. Don't be a crying baby. Don't trouble your mother." With this last statement, the ceremony is finished, and all those present join together and partake of the meat.

The relationship between the spiritual entity reincarnating the child and the child itself is not well defined. Although reincarnated, the child is believed to have no knowledge of any prior existence except for what he is told by other people. Reincarnation appears to occur in a random fashion. The only apparent relationship occurs between the class of spirits called *tome* and the future development of the child's interests and abilities. Thus, a child reincarnated by the "xylophone spirit" (*luri tome*) will tend to develop interests in the direction of xylophone playing. The same applies to spirits relating to hunting (*tome*), divining (*vuruga tome*), and blacksmithing (*lukuru tome*). This relationship is not a necessary one, however, for one's specialization of interest in these directions is largely determined by a secondary reincarnation or "marriage" which occurs during later childhood or adolescence.

The relationship of reincarnation to birth is better understood in terms of the relationship of the *janwuo* to the supernatural world. Three factors are closely interrelated: the birth of children, the wealth and goodness of the people, and the power of the ancestors and other supernatural entities which protect the people. The Sisala often say, "This house has a very powerful shrine (*vene, tome,* or *dalusun*) because it has reincarnated many children in this house," or "There are many children in this house named after such and such an ancestor." The fact that a *janwuo* has many children attests to the fact that the spiritual deities belonging to the *janwuo* are powerful. On the other hand, it is believed that the "community of the dead" (*lelejang*) is largely a reflection of the "community of the living" (*jang*). Again the Sisala say, "I cannot do what my father has not done." If, for example, the ancestors of an extended family or clan section are evil and their previous deeds on earth were characterized by internal dissention or even homicide, this condition will be reflected in the present state of family affairs and over a period of time the *janwuo* would split apart and be destroyed. Conversely, if the ancestors and other supernatural entities of a people are good and powerful and if the people take care to behave in the ways prescribed by the ancestors, the maintenance of this proper relationship will be rewarded by the fertility of women and a growth in the size and wealth of the family.

The belief in reincarnation and its representation in the naming ceremony is a symbolic nexus representing the "alpha" (the phenomenon of birth and the community of the living) and the "omega" (the world of the dead and the supernatural). The child's position in the social and supernatural order has now been established; as he grows up, he will be taught to understand the nature of this order in which he has been ordained to live.

INFANCY: BIRTH TO THREE YEARS

The infant receives constant care, attention, and love from all members of the extended family. He is almost always in the company of his mother, though others, especially the father, are often seen fondling the child. The Sisala say that a baby has no "sense" (*wijima*) and is not able to take care of himself; inherent in the notion of *wijima* is the idea of knowing right from wrong. The baby can do no evil and therefore can be loved and indulged without fear of his being spoiled.

When asked why they demonstrate such care for their babies, the Sisala often reply that a baby is weak by nature and susceptible to illnesses and to the malevolent designs of witches. Therefore, close attention must be paid to him lest he fall ill and die. Sisala babies and small children often wear a wide variety of protective charms and amulets, the specific nature of which is determined either by family tradition or by consulting a diviner. Many children wear a charm about their necks which consists of a coin in the shape of the moon, for it is believed that if a baby's face looks toward the moon, especially during the lunar cycle in which it was born, his face will become deeply furrowed and he will resemble a monkey. Protective charms, usually consisting of cowrie shells, are given to the child by the mother's brother. Since cowrie shells are symbolic of wealth, this charm is given to insure that the baby remains fat and healthy.

The beliefs concerning the weaknesses and innocence of babies are paralleled by indulgent practices of child care and early training. All babies are breast-fed, and there are no fixed times for feeding. Whenever the child cries or expresses the slightest discomfort, the mother offers her breast to give the baby an object to play with or to quiet the child and encourage him to sleep. In the latter case the offering of the breast is often accompanied by a gentle rocking motion of the mother or by her singing lullabies.

The child's reaction to feeding is regarded by the Sisala as the best index of its general state of health. If the child persists in crying after he is fed or if he refuses to nurse, the mother worries about his health and may consult a *hachikuoro* in order to discover the cause of the problem. It is believed that the most common cause of loss of appetite is constipation, in which case the *hachikuoro* will prescribe a purgative to free the baby's bowels. If this measure does not succeed, the father takes charge of the matter and consults a diviner to determine the cause.

In these cases of seemingly discontented children, the fault is often believed to lie with the mother. Throughout the nursing period sexual intercourse is absolutely forbidden. If it should take place, it is believed that the mother's milk will turn sour and cause the child to have frequent bowel movements, often resulting in death. It is also believed that during pregnancy the ancestors and various spiritual deities worshipped by the husband's *janwuo* come in human form as strangers to test the character of the pregnant woman. They will usually ask for food, water, or something which they are sure the woman can provide, and if they are refused, her milk will become insufficient. In both cases sacrifices to the appropriate deities must be performed to insure the safety of the child.

Weaning is a gradual process spread over a period of three years. At eight months the child is introduced to a light porridge prepared from millet flour and water, and adult foods such as *kulung* (a thickened form of millet flour food), yams, and beans are subsequently given. Throughout this period, however, until the age of three, children are encouraged to continue feeding from their mother's breast. If the child stops nursing voluntarily, he is not forced to continue, but if at three years he continues to nurse, the mother applies some bitter herbs to the breast.

Toilet training begins at the age of one-and-a-half. Prior to this time nothing is done to encourage habits of continence, and if the baby urinates or defecates in the mother's lap, she simply cleans herself and pays no further attention to the matter. By the time the child is one-and-a-half to two years of age, he is expected to report to his mother when it needs to eliminate. When he does so, the mother asks a sibling to direct the child outside the house. When the infant returns, the mother washes him with water and a piece of cloth. At this time also the mother begins to wake the child in the middle of the night and take it outside to urinate. Such training prevents the habit of night wetting. If after the age of three the child continues to soil his mother's clothing or eliminate in the house, he is punished by his mother.

Toilet training is not characterized by any strong value placed upon cleanliness or by any sentiment akin to disgust or repugnance. Since water was traditionally a scarce commodity in the area, especially during the dry season, bathing was largely regarded as a luxury. Small livestock such as fowls, goats and sheep are kept within the walls of the *janwuo* making insignificant the excrement of one small child. On one occasion, upon seeing a baby excrete in its mother's lap, I asked the mother whether she was upset by what the child had done. She replied that on the contrary, she regarded herself as fortunate to have a child to soil her clothes. Toilet training and sphincter control, like so many aspects of child training, are seen in terms of the expectation of normal behavior: what is expected of a child at any point in his life is determined by his capacities and interests at that time.

The expectation of normal behavior applies especially to the early training in motor skills. From the time of birth to the age of three the infant is in the constant presence of people who fulfill his needs. Although the average Sisala child appears quite capable of walking between the ages of one and two, he is seldom encouraged to do so. When the mother wishes to travel or to go out in public, she binds the child to her back with his feet straddling her waist. Between the ages of two and three, the child is usually carried in an informal manner straddling the mother's hip. The same manner of transportation is used when the child is placed in the care of elder siblings or cousins. When the child is not being carried, he is allowed to crawl about and explore within the house, but again the mother pays constant attention to the child lest it hurt himself. Any mother who encourages her infant to walk prior to the normal development of such skills is ridiculed by the other women in the *janwuo,* who frequently say that she is impatient for her child to grow up so she can have sexual intercourse again.

It should not be concluded, however, that the infant's life is relegated to motor inactivity. Parents merely feel it is wrong to train or encourage a child of this age to grow up; instead, small children are meant to be played with. They are believed to be friendly by nature and loving of company. When the mother and father have free time, they often sit and play with the child. It is a common sight to see a mother lying on the mat in her room rolling about with a baby and letting it crawl over her. When the parents are busy with their work, the infant is often left in the care of a grandparent

Mothers and their children in the inner yard of the janwuo.

who is regarded as the child's "playmate." Thus, the infant's psychomotor development is shaped in a setting of playful interaction.

In sum, this period from birth to three years may be described as one of indulgence, characterized by the constant presence of human caretakers, watchfulness, concern for the child's condition, responsiveness to the immediate needs of the child, absence of corporal punishment, and lack of stress upon achievement, responsibility, and compliance. These characteristic patterns of infant rearing are very similar to those employed by Barry, Bacon, and Child (1957) to define "overall infant indulgence," and by their criteria, the Sisala would receive a high rating. It is worthwhile, however, to examine two basic theories of development which pertain to the importance of the first three years in the establishment of personality trends or dispositions.

The first of these theories is stated succinctly by Whiting *et al.* in the form of a hypothesis: "Indulgence in infancy will tend to produce (a) a trustful attitude toward others, (b) general optimism, and (c) sociability (1966:14)." Erikson expresses similar conclusions:

> The first demonstration of social trust in the baby is the ease of his feeding, the depth of his sleep, the relaxation of his bowels. The experience of mutual regulation of his increasingly receptive capacities with the maternal techniques of provision gradually helps him balance the discomfort caused by the immaturity of homeostasis with which he is born. . . . The infant's first social achievement, then, is his willingness to let the mother out of sight without undue anxiety or rage, because she has become an inner certainty as well as an outer predictability (1950:247).

The fact that the Sisala mother is constantly with the child, responding to his immediate needs and placing few inhibitions upon his physiological development, tends to support Erikson. Although it is difficult to determine the presence of trust in Sisala infants, the belief on the part of adults that babies are lovable and a joy to be with serves to reinforce this notion.

The question of the disposition toward sociability is somewhat easier to examine. In a crosscultural study by Barry, Bacon, and Child (1957) a high positive correlation between the size of households and the amount of "overall infant indulgence" was found. This was explained by the fact that in nuclear family households the infant is often left alone for long periods of time while the mother is engaged in her everyday tasks. In large extended families, on the other hand, more hands are available to take care of the child, and the infant is seldom left to rely upon himself. Under these conditions not only are the needs of the infant met more consistently, but the affective attachments of the child are more diffuse, extending in principle to all of the members of the extended family. Thus, the indulgence of the infant by many socializing agents tends to affect the child's eventual disposition to sociability. While it is again difficult to determine the degree of infant sociability among the Sisala, it may be noted that Sisala households, according to the 1960 Ghana census, are the largest in all Ghana and that the criteria cited by Barry, Bacon, and Child pertaining to indulgence and sociability also apply to the Sisala. Also the fact that the Sisala infant is believed to be dependent and in need of attention and the fact that parents enjoy stimulating the infant to play are related to the developing of a predisposition to sociability.

The second theoretical position concerning the problem of indulgence is best represented in the writings of McClelland (1961) and McClelland and Friedman (1952) on achievement motivation and personality autonomy. They state that children with a high disposition toward achievement and autonomy are those who during their infancy underwent severe independence training. Among the characteristics of independence training are early weaning, the granting of freedom to the infant to structure his own time and activities (for example, a child playing by himself in a playpen), the encouragement of the infant to perform tasks and motor skills prior to the time of his physiological maturation, and the imposition of standards of excellence on the infant's performances of tasks and skills. McClelland's use of the word "severe" is not synonymous with punishing; rather it means that a greater demand is placed upon the infant to rely upon himself and to learn to achieve in terms of his own abilities instead of relying on others. Hagen (1962) further suggests that when an infant is encouraged to perform a task beyond his natural ability, he suffers from anxiety caused by his physical insecurity. If, however, the infant is lovingly rewarded for his attempts and successes, this pattern of anxiety followed by reward will create a long-lasting and powerful motivating force. He continues:

> On balance, the individual who has had this kind of experience in early childhood anticipates success each time he tries to achieve in later life, for this was the pattern of early striving; but because success is not a foregone conclusion, he forever feels a need to try another task and reassure himself (Hagen 1962:141).

Early Sisala training does not contribute to the development of autonomy and achievement. In an environment where the infant's needs are immediately satisfied and where he is not encouraged to perform motor tasks beyond its ability, little need exists for the infant to structure his environment or to act independently of others. Instead, parental attitudes concerning the dependency and innate warmth of infants reinforce behavioral dispositions in the direction of sociability and affective dependence.

EARLY CHILDHOOD: THREE TO SIX YEARS

The period between three and six years may be characterized at best as transitional. Upon weaning, the child is considered too old to be indulged and played with "by heart" (that is, with abandon, without constraint), yet especially in the case of a male child, he is not old enough to have "sense" (*wijima*) or to be useful.

More than any other factor, pregnancy and the arrival of a new baby determine the time when weaning will occur, and this process is gradual and without trauma. Yet as a social phenomenon it has deeper significance since it involves the withdrawal of the mother's indulgent protection and the very real awareness on the part of the child of a sibling competitor. Instead of being the recipient of protective indulgence, the child must now learn to give it to the newly born younger sibling.

A ceremony marks the end of this gradual weaning process and signifies the beginning of the child's new relationships within the family. This event takes place soon after the birth of the new child and involves the mother and the recently weaned child or that child nearest in age to the new baby. When the room is cleared of afterbirth and blood, the *hachikuoro* attending the mother boils an egg. Having the child stand before the door of the room where the new baby is lying, she places the egg on his head and allows it to drop to the ground. The child is then told to pick it up and eat it. As he eats it, he is informed that he is now grown and has a brother or sister and that he must be kind to the little one. He is also told that he likes babies and that is why he allowed his mother to have one. He is then allowed to see his newly arrived younger sibling.

With this ceremony the child embarks upon another stage of his life, the stage in which he begins to form basic relationships which will endure throughout his life. The social environment within which these relationships are formed is the extended family and at times the minor lineage. The term "father" (*nyimma*), for example, applies not only to one's biological father but also to the father's brothers and in its widest context to any patrilineally related male of the ascending generation. The word "mother" (*nang*) includes the child's biological mother, the mother's sisters, the mother's cowives, and the father's brother's wives. Lastly, the terms for brother, *ngana* or "junior sibling" and *mallma* or "senior sibling," apply to biological siblings, father's brother's children, and by extension to all patrilineally related males of the same generation. To view the socialization process in terms of nuclear family relationships would be misleading since what the child learns during this period is how to relate to classes of people within the extended family and minor lineage. As he grows older, he comes to generalize the principles learned in this limited setting to situations in the broader society.

Let us now turn to an examination of the enculturative process in terms of the child's relationships within the extended family.

Between the ages of three and five the child begins to see his mother not merely as a source of nurturant protection but also as a *nang* or "mother" among the other "mothers" of the extended family. The disappointments and frustrations inherent in this period of adjustment help to create a conceptualization of women which forms an enduring impression in the mind of the male child as he grows into adulthood. The girl child has an easier adjustment since she remains close to her mother, beginning at an early age to help her mother with the daily tasks of a woman.

By any objective standard, the young wife-mother occupies a "deprived" position in the male-oriented Sisala culture. When a woman marries, she must give up the favored position as "daughter" and "sister" in her father's house and take on the initially unrewarding roles as wife and mother. Until she becomes older and past the age of childbearing, the status of the wife-mother is determined solely by her ability to bear children and care for them in their early years. The barren woman is a disgrace to herself and the subject of ridicule by the other women in the *janwuo*. Although being barren is not in itself a sufficient cause for divorce, it is an important contributing factor, since a woman who is ridiculed and caused to lose face often leaves her husband. Also it is believed that a barren woman may be evil and that her evil and quarrelsome nature is reflected in her poor behavior as a wife.

This emphasis upon childbearing in a male-oriented society affects the mother's attitude toward her own children. The presence of the small baby is a source of great pleasure for the mother. Especially during the time of her first child when she may feel somewhat a stranger in her husband's house, the baby provides the mother with company, someone she can indulge and play with. Also the infant is a sign of prestige, a symbol which the mother proudly carries in public and which attests to her value as a woman. On the other hand, as the *pose* or "pouring" [water] ceremony demonstrates, the child belongs to the father, and the young wife realizes that if she leaves her husband, she must also leave her children. Although women are very reluctant to express dissatisfaction with their state of affairs, on one occasion an educated woman criticized her brother, saying, "You men! Somebody [referring to the author] would think from the way you talk that it is you rather than we women who give birth to children. When our children are sick, we are the ones who sit up through the night. Yet you take the credit for curing their illnesses."

Thus, the mother fondles her child as her own while realizing that the child is not hers and that someday he will leave her protection. This creates an ambivalent attitude which is seen most strongly in the mother's relationship with her growing infant son. In interviews mothers demonstrated a definite preference for younger infants and a general disaffection as they perceive the baby growing older. The older child is seen as heavier to carry, not as much fun to play with, and more troublesome about the house. A female child is favored by the mother since she will help her with the tasks about the house and provide her with companionship; the male child, on the other hand, will eventually grow up and prefer the father. As the male infant grows into childhood, the mother tells him not to bother her, saying such things as, "Be like your father," or "This is something a boy your age doesn't do."

A boy begins to detect the mother's dissatisfaction during her next pregnancy. The Sisala say that a pregnant woman is like a cat because she wants nothing to do with her own children. When the child realizes the reason for his mother's estrangement, his reaction is often violent. He may run away from his mother's house and refuse to return, preferring to stay with his father or father's brother. After the baby is born, he may tell his mother or others in the *janwuo* that they should send the newly born baby away or have it killed. Verbal behavior of this sort and the temper tantrums which often accompany it are regarded as intolerable by parents and punishment is severe. It is felt that if such blatant acts of disrespect are allowed to continue, the boy will grow up to be a "useless child" (*bichuola*) who will show no respect for his elders and will quarrel continually with his brothers. The child's emotional reaction to the mother's withdrawal of indulgence serves to reinforce her attitude that he will become troublesome and capable of malice, and therefore can no longer be the object of unconstrained love.

While the mother directs her attention to the baby, the newly weaned child goes to live temporarily with another woman in the *janwuo*, usually the mother's cowife or the father's brother's wife, both of whom have children of their own. While previously the infant ate with his mother, he now eats from a common plate with siblings and is expected to exhibit manners. He begins to perceive himself as merely another child of the family. Even though he is allowed to sleep in his mother's room, he no longer occupies the privileged position by his mother's side which is now relinquished to his younger sibling.

This dramatic introduction of a younger sibling into the experience of the child leads to the realization of his role as a sibling and his position in the birth order. To his younger brother (*ngana*), he is expected to be kind and protective; to his elder brother (*mallma*), he is expected to be obedient and dependent. While a boy refers to his sister by the term *dihaala*, no single term is used for "brother." The reverse is true for girls; her brother is always *dibaala*, while her sisters are either *ngana* "younger sister" or *mallma* "older sister." This emphasis upon relative seniority in the kinship terms for siblings and cousins of the same sex is significant in understanding the subsequent role relationships among siblings.

Although the three-year-old is not deemed mature enough to assume protective responsibilities for his younger sibling, he is expected to show him loving kindness. It is a common sight to see a mother nursing and fondling her baby while one of her younger children looks on. While the mother may pretend not to notice the older child, the latter may attempt to gain the mother's attention by smiling at the baby or by making other loving gestures. On one occasion while a father was sitting with his five-year-old son, the small baby he was holding began to play with the boy. Although the baby hit him and gouged at his eyes, the father merely looked on laughingly while the older child patiently forced a smile. The sincerity of this expression of loving affection is doubtful. On another occasion, I observed a five-year-old girl playing with her younger brother of about two years. She began biting the infant gently on the stomach, causing him to laugh, but when no one was looking, she bit down hard upon his umbilical hernia, causing the infant to cry. The mother then came and picked up the child while the older sister stood by with a look of assumed innocence.

The central aspect of sibling relations from the viewpoint of the young child is play. Since the mother is usually busy caring for her baby or engaging in other work, the care of the young child is entrusted to an older sibling. The children of the minor lineage congregate and play with one another in the outside yard (*biling*) of the minor lineage settlement. Although unstructured activities, such as running and wrestling, do exist, the majority of the play is structured in terms of specific pastimes and games within the relational context of siblings and patrilineally related cousins.

Much of girls' play closely resembles the Western idea of "playing house." Older girls pretend to prepare millet by substituting sand and grinding it between two small stones, while others imitate such womanly pursuits as making porridge and gathering firewood and water. These imitations are miniaturizations of the technical and social aspects of the adult economic routine, and thus the small head braces used by girls to carry firewood are almost identical to those used by adult women for the same purpose. The organization and distribution of tasks is also similar to that of the adult extended family with the older girls assuming the positions of senior wives, while the younger ones act as their junior wives. Those girls without younger siblings frequently fashion dolls out of sticks of wood and carry them on their backs with the support of a cloth wrapping.

While girls imitate the activities of their "mothers," boys imitate those of their "fathers." Small boys gather sand and pretend to make a yam mound using a groundnut wrapped in leaves as the seed yam and later harvesting it. Boys also pretend to be hunters, the younger ones walking on all fours imitating the actions of antelopes or water buffaloes, while the older ones run after them pretending to shoot them with bows and arrows. After they "kill" their game, they carry the small child home for a hunting dance. As in the case of girls, the roles in these games are determined by relative seniority, and the younger boy frequently ends up in the least desirable role.

It should also be noted that the play activities of boys and girls often intersect. When the girls play house, the boys sometimes bring food which they have supposedly grown on the farm. The girls "prepare" it, and both pretend to partake in a meal. These pastimes may achieve a high level of complexity as when children of both sexes pretend to perform a funeral. A lizard is usually killed and placed against some small sticks in a manner similar to the way the corpse is displayed at a Sisala burial. Various roles such as those of the xylophone players, *bukaliba* ("those who bury the dead"), and praise singers are assumed by the children, and some of the funeral dances are performed. The older children, from six to ten years, may also play husband and wife, but if this kind of activity leads to sex play, corporal punishment is severe since any kind of sexual expression among "siblings" of the minor lineage is regarded as incestuous. Children may play together as husband and wife, but only in the purely economic aspects of these roles.

While parents regard an interest in children's play beneath their dignity, they are nonetheless concerned that their children remain orderly and not fight. The Sisala are fully aware that their children will eventually grow up to succeed the authority of the senior generation and to inherit its property. Divisiveness exhibited during childhood is carefully observed as reflecting future problems and conflicts, for the Sisala say that when brothers fight as children, they will fight as adults. Unlike the arguments of childhood, however, such divisiveness later in life would threaten the unity and continuity of the *janwuo.*

Thus, parents instruct older children to care for their younger siblings and to encourage them to participate in the playful activities of the other children. If a small child of three or four years is seen playing by himself, the parents reprimand the older sibling for not caring for his younger brother or sister. When quarrels break out, the father and mother are careful to listen to both sides of the argument in order to affect a resolution. Blame is usually placed on the older child who is believed to have "sense" and be capable of thinking "bad thoughts." In cases where the fault obviously lies with the small child, the parent reminds the older one that his younger brother does not know better and that he should be understanding and patient.

Aside from infrequent parental intervention the play activities of children are entirely the province of children, and within this play environment the small child comes to perceive the sociocultural world in terms of his elder brother's playful interpretation of adult activities. The learning process is both diffuse and gradual. It is diffuse in the sense that every elder male child in the minor lineage constitutes a possible perspective for male identification; it is gradual in that the primary source of identification is a sibling rather than a parent. As a passive observer the small child's needs are cared for and his time is structured; social cooperation is emphasized and little stress is placed upon the need for creative initiative in the development of the child's interests. And as the child reaches the age of six, he becomes a senior sibling in the context of the play group, thus taking on the role of caretaker and teacher of his younger brother.

As is the case with the mother, the three-year-old perceives its loss of favor with the father. This is a greater problem with a boy than for a girl. Although the girl is always with her mother, learning the simple tasks about the house, a boy does not occupy a similar useful position in relation to the father or the father's brothers. Rather, he is expected to busy himself with childish things and not to bother older people while they are working. Inquisitive efforts and attempts to secure indulgence are discouraged. The child is merely expected to grow up, and except for a few perfunctory "dos" and "don'ts" little attention is given to his educational development.

When this distant and somewhat austere relationship with the father is seen in connection with the separation and loss of maternal indulgence, it is clear that a generalized feeling of anxiety is caused in the small child by the insecurity of its status. Anxiety during this period is reflected in answers given by children concerning memorable childhood experiences. Many recall frightful incidents during early childhood years such as encounters with ghosts (*kokong*) and witnessing childbirth and death.

The following is typical of a response, and it concerns a boy's remembrance of a funeral performance.

> One morning when I was asleep in my father's compound, I could hear some people beating drums and some singing wild songs. As a small child, I got up at once and I could find nobody in the room. So I ran out to see what was happening. And when I went out, I saw that there was no other small boy there but me. When I went near them, I saw one man in front of them [the singers] keeping a goat in his mouth and sucking the blood and eating the raw meat. When I saw that, I thought that the goat was a boy so I quickly ran to find my mother. And when I was running, I thought they were trying to eat me too. So I went and hid myself thinking I wouldn't be seen. I could still hear the wild songs, and I didn't know where to go, so I went out of my hiding place. I then saw my own mother coming towards me, but I thought she was coming to eat me up. So I was running again and she was calling me and when I turned to look at her, she showed me a mango.

Anxiety in children is caused not only by the withdrawal of protective indulgence but also by exposure to frightening events which parents do not endeavor to explain to their children. Many adult Sisala laughingly recall such incidents saying that "small boys" frighten easily. Parents also feel that it is important for a child to learn to "fear (*fa*) his father" and to "fear the ancestors" for a "child who does not fear his father will not respect him." At the funeral place, for example, when "man songs" (*bayila*) are sung and war dances performed, it is a common sight to see a man lurch out at the onlooking children with his battle axe and to see the children running away crying hysterically. In short, the child comes to fear his father and the "male culture" associated with him as being potentially unpredictable and dangerous.

Although the father is perceived as an object to be feared, he is also seen by the child as a protector, as the means by which his fears may be ameliorated. The following statements concerning childhood experiences emphasize this point.

> I was sleeping in my father's room when I heard a knocking at the door. When I woke, I heard somebody calling my father. I was only five years old then. It was 12 o'clock in the night. I opened the door and it came inside. When I saw the man, I knew it was a ghost (*kokong*). So I hid myself in the corner. It began to go toward my sister. And so I cried and shouted, "Who is that?" My father got up and gave it a blow and it went away. Round about 1:30 in the night, it came again. My father is a hunter, so he took a knife and slaughtered it. Then in a minute, it disappeared for good.

A second experience is related by a girl.

> The childhood experience I remember most took place in my father's house. I was only five years old. And in my childhood, I was very troublesome. It happened one day that in the evening when my mother was cooking, I went to sit by the fire. Immediately after she finished cooking, the fire was red hot and I thought it was something nice so I went inside the fire and my whole body was burned. I gave a loud cry and my mother ran to take me out of the fire. My father was sitting outside in the yard. He came in and shouted at my mother and carried me inside the house. During this time I was sore and my father was all the time in the house. He worried and thought I would die, but to my fortune I recovered and he is now back to work again.

Both of these recollections demonstrate that in time of danger and illness it is the father rather than the mother who is perceived as the source of protection. One reason for this may stem from the child's realization that it is only the father who is in possession of the supernatural means for curing illness (*dalusun* or "medicines") and for ritually managing the contingent and fearful world. When a child falls sick, the father consults a diviner to determine the cause of illness, and he administers the cure. It is the father whom the child sees performing sacrifices to the shrines in the house in order to insure the protection of the ancestors and the blessings of wealth and prosperity. The father, who on the one hand is the object of fear, is on the other the person who must be depended upon in time of danger. These ambivalent attitudes are also characteristic of the Sisala's view of the ancestors, and in the child's eyes then the father's order is a miniature of the larger socioreligious order which the child eventually comes to learn.

CHILDHOOD: SIX TO TEN YEARS

Central to the parents' attitude toward the growing child during this period is the notion of "sense" or "knowing things" (*wijima*). When the child reaches the age of six years, he is expected to know the difference between right and wrong and to begin assuming minor responsibilities by contributing his labor to the common economic pursuits of the *janwuo*. One elder man summarized the idea of *wijima* in the following way:

> When a child is a bit grown, you give him jobs to do. If the child idles about, when he grows up, he will be an idle person. A boy of about six years of age does not have the "sense" of a grown-up. But he should know what is right and what is wrong. A boy who has "sense" can explain things well to his elders. Such a boy can sit with his elder brothers and understand what they are saying. He remembers things when he is told. A child who tries to know more than his father is a "useless child" (*bichuola*), for he has no respect. Also, *wijima* means clever. If, for example, a boy sees that his father is without matches, he will run and get them without being asked.

The notion of "sense" is a comprehensive one related to almost all aspects of the child's experience. It applies to the parents' attitude toward the child and to the child's awareness and perception of the parental generation as a group to be feared and respected. It also applies to the nature of the learning process itself. This concept, therefore, is to be regarded as central to the subsequent discussion of the educational process and social development of the child.

When a child reaches the age of five or six, he usually begins to express an interest in accompanying his father to the farm or going with elder brothers to help graze the livestock. He demonstrates his interest by economic play activities and by asking to use his father's farming implements. Parents say that their small children often cry when they are not allowed to accompany their fathers and brothers to the farm. Fathers regard these kinds of behavior as a good sign, for it means that such children will grow up to be useful and hard working. When it is felt that his abilities warrant his interests, the child is assigned simple tasks to perform.

The development of the child's interests and the manner in which he is trained must be understood within the context of the extended family or *janwuo*. As an economically corporate group its members participate together in common economic pursuits. The adult male productive unit consists not only of the father but also the father's brothers. Concerning the relationship of the parental and child generations, the Sisala have a proverb (*namaka*) which states, "Your children are your brother's children and your brother's children are your children." When asked about the meaning of the proverb, the Sisala say that a *janwuo* will break up when brothers quarrel; in order to prevent this and to maintain a unified *janwuo*, they believe that a father cannot be selfish about his own children at the expense of his brother's children. This means that a boy is often trained by his father's brother rather than by his father. Many factors determine such a relationship, most of them idiosyncratic. If, for example, a child demonstrates an interest in hunting, he may develop a close relationship with one of his father's brothers who is a hunter. This "father" then serves as the child's primary teacher not only in hunting but also in the acquisition of other necessary knowledge and skills. Similar dictates of interest serve as determinants in the formation of relationships with the children of one's father's brothers.

The effect of this custom on the child's subsequent educational experience is to create in his mind a primary awareness of himself as a member of an extended family and only a secondary valuation on his affiliation with a nuclear family subunit. Thus, in everyday conversation the term "father" (*nyimma*) as any male member of the ascending generation within the *janwuo* is more significant than the notion of father as a single person.

Except in very large families where occupational specializations such as hunting are full time vocations, the boy is expected to demonstrate an interest in both farming and herding. The relative emphasis given to either of these activities depends upon the child's interests and seasonally defined work requirements. When a small boy first goes to the farm with his father, he is told to sit in the shade of a tree and observe what his elders are doing. When he asks to help, someone gives him a hoe with which to play. As the boy's persistence increases, he is allocated a few minor chores such as gathering white ants and grass to feed the poultry, or frightening crows feeding on the crops. He is also expected to help those who work by running for water and when older, building a fire and preparing the midday meal. The child learns herding from his elder "brothers" by accompanying them to the outskirts of the village where together they graze the sheep and cattle. Though the hours are long, most of the time is spent sitting beneath the trees playing games. Children from other villages often graze livestock in the same area, and they may gather together to tell stories. As with farming, the boy is expected to run errands and help prepare meals for his older brothers.

Girls assume work responsibilities at an earlier age, possibly stemming from the fact that a girl's duties, like those of her mother, are carried out either within or in close proximity to the compound while a boy must await the time he is physically able to walk the distance to the farm or to where the livestock is grazed. When she is about four years old, the girl is assigned useful tasks such as sweeping the compound yard and carrying small pots of water from a nearby water hole. Small girls are also entrusted with the care of babies and infants while their mothers are engaged in other activities. At about six years the girl begins helping with the preparation of food, though it is not until she is older that she is allowed to prepare food by herself. Unlike men's work which is organized and carried out as enterprise of the entire *janwuo*, women's work is organized in terms of each nuclear or polygynous household unit. The mother and father's other wives, along with the elder sisters, are the young girl's teachers.

The educational process is best described as situational; that is, the child acquires a competence in the knowledge and skills of his culture in the context of everyday practical situations. When a small boy learns to use a hoe, he does so first by observing his father on the farm and then by experimenting on a small plot of land. The father does not think of sitting down with his son and explicitly teaching him the use of a hoe. Rather, the child is expected to carefully observe his elders in their everyday routine, and as he develops an interest and begins experimenting the father gives him instructions. The boy is expected to learn the particular skill the first time it is explained to him. If he fails to utilize the new knowledge, his father becomes annoyed, for the Sisala believe that a child who does not learn readily when young will be lazy and useless when an adult.

Young boys practice the xylophone while their fathers are away.

The following statement exemplifies well the role of situational observation in the Sisala educational process. It was given by a boy of about thirteen years of age.

> When I was six years old, I started experiencing life. During this time I had a very small mind for thinking, but it thought many things. There were many questions which I asked my father and my brother but they would not answer them. One day I asked my father how a child learns to speak and he said that I should be playing with small children and watching them. . . .

> One day I came to the house and sat by a small child crying for his mother. His mother came and took him and was bathing him. The mother then talked to the child and he became quiet. So then I knew a small child can tell the voice of his mother . . . After that I was always with the woman and one day I saw the child say "m--ma" which means mother. Getting to some time I got to know that the boy speaks only with the mother, but when he sees somebody near, he will not speak . . . One day I was resting with my older brother and the baby was brought in by the mother. My brother then said "*ko*" which means "come" in Sisala. The baby then stretched out his arms and my brother collected him. Then my brother said that a child learns from the mother first, and then from the father.

This emphasis upon situational observation and the lack of formal or structured learning is characteristic of all aspects of the enculturative process, especially the learning of family and tribal traditions. It should be noted here that there is no aspect of Sisala adult culture which is concealed from children. Whether it be a religious performance or a heated dispute between two elder men, children are allowed to gather and observe. In the evening after dinner the children in the *janwuo* listen to their fathers while they discuss events of the day. Folktale sessions take place in the evenings, and during these times—especially during times of intravillage conflict and dispute—various *namaka* or "true stories" are cited.

A high value is attached to listening and observation, and a child who does not listen or who asks unnecessary questions is regarded as "useless" (*chuola*). Frequently the elder men question the children afterward to see how well they listened, and those who did not listen, or those "useless" children who chose to sit with their mothers, are punished. On one occasion in the village of Sorbelle the elder men of the extended families of one of the clan sections met together to prepare a case to defend the right of one of their members to hold the position of chieftain in the village. For more than three hours they cited various clan and family traditions, and women, children, and young adults listened attentively. One young man remarked afterwards that much of what he heard that day was new to him and that he regarded himself fortunate to have been present to hear these things.

In sum, greater expectations are made of the child in accordance with the perceived state of his physical development or age. Rather than formally structuring the learning process, the parent expects the child to demonstrate an interest in the ongoing activities of the household, and the older the child becomes, the greater becomes the pressure upon him to develop or to acquire a mastery of his culture.

The increased pressures upon learning and compliance reflect the greater importance and seriousness of the economic tasks assigned to the child, and thus he is never entrusted with any task beyond his abilities. Although the initial jobs given to a small child are relatively unimportant, his conscientious performance of them serves as a basis for entrusting him with more important responsibilities. If a boy is careless and allows his father's livestock to wander off into the bush, he is punished severely, but by listening carefully to the instructions of his father and brothers and by obeying them unquestioningly, the child is rewarded with work assignments concommitant with his father's perception of his abilities.

With these social responsibilities comes an awareness on the part of the child of his usefulness. When questioned, children frequently speak in terms of "our cattle," "our millet," or "our ancestors." And when asked why they enjoy working on the farm or herding livestock, they reply that if no one (including themselves) worked, the family would starve. When a small boy helps his fathers gather clay in order to make mortar for bricks, he perceives the instrumental importance of his work in terms of his partial contribution to the building of a house. While on the one hand he performs his task, on the other he is observing the work activities of the senior male members of the house. And while he is aware of his limitations at any particular stage of his development, he is also able to perceive his eventual role as an adult. Thus, his awareness of the instrumental importance of his knowledge, and his ability to envision the ends of the educational process in terms of his social usefulness, clearly make the learning process a meaningful experience and provide a strong incentive to grow up.

As we have seen, the value attached to children is based almost solely upon the criterion of usefulness. A child who has *wijima* and exhibits social responsibility is regarded as useful; conversely, a child without sense is "useless." However, the sense of a child is not the same as that of an adult, for the Sisala say that a child has a mind which is "small for learning." An elder man also has *wijima,* but in this case the word translates as "wisdom" or "knowing of the deeper things." The educational process, as perceived by the Sisala, is essentially a one-way transaction between the infinitely wiser parental generation and the gradually developing child generation. In order that this relationship be maintained, the Sisala insist that children learn the proper behavior and the correct manner of relating to adult authority.

The Sisala believe that children are by nature incapable of placing internal demands upon themselves. Beginning at about the age of three years with the occurrence of temper tantrums, the child is perceived as being capable of unkindness or evil. When he reaches the age of six and is said to have acquired "sense," he is seen as capable of differentiating between right and wrong. Parents believe that if a child is left to act by himself, he will steal, argue, fight, and act mischievously. In other words, the child knows enough to be bad but not enough to be good. Children between the ages of six and ten are kept under constant supervision by the various adult members of the *janwuo.* They are not allowed to roam unaccompanied to the other minor lineage settlements in the village, because children of this age are seldom concerned about the prestige of their family and might therefore start fights, beg food, or in other ways disgrace their families. If a child does exhibit model behavior, this is taken as a natural function of the growth process, and he is not praised or rewarded by his parents for doing what is expected of him.

In sum, although the child is in possession of "sense," it is believed that he is unwilling to make any demands upon himself; therefore, he must be taught basic rules of respect for one's elders and respect for their property. The notion of "respect" is expressed by two related concepts: *fa* or "fearful respect" and *zile* or "politeness, mutual respect."

The Sisala believe that a boy must be made to fear (*fa*) his father. As noted earlier, the child begins developing fears in early childhood as a reaction to his perception of the father and the male culture. Parents often encourage the formation of such fears through the use of childhood fictions, and teasing children provides adults with a source of entertainment. One man remarked to me that as a child he was in the habit of urinating frequently in the evenings. One night his father told him that if he went outside to urinate in the night, a big lizard would come and bite off his penis. He still expresses great fear of lizards. This general state of anxiety created through the use of fictions and parental teasing is expressed in irrational fears of animals such as the lizard, toad, and the now almost extinct lion.

When a Sisala man is asked why a son should show fear toward his father, he often replies by saying, "If a man doesn't fear his father, who then will he fear?" To show fear in the presence of authority is therefore regarded as a positive virtue, and training in bravery, physical endurance, or independence would be considered absurd, for a child so raised would become "full of pride" and lacking in respect for age. When addressing his father, a boy is expected to lower his eyes while his father stares at him directly. Whereas a boy may speak freely with his brothers, he must approach his father in an indirect manner; rather than telling his father what is on his mind, he often waits until his father addresses him or guesses the nature of his problem or question. If the father is in a bad mood or angry, the boy makes every effort to avoid him.

In the same way that a child fears his father, he fears being punished. If he does something wrong, he is warned by his father who says that if he does such a thing again, he will be punished. Parents believe that if one shouts at a child when warning him, he will come to fear his father and therefore act properly. The Sisala regard as ludicrous a child who would admit to having committed a wrong and who would bravely stand up to receive his punishment. In fact, admission of this sort would border on disrespect since the expected reaction in the presence of someone in authority would be silence and evasion. If a child commits an act for which he knows he will be punished, he often avoids or hides from his father, hoping that the father's (or father's brother's) temper will cool. When confronted by the father, the boy is expected to lie or at least not to admit his actions. In punishing the child, then, the father must depend upon others in the house to report to him what the child has done. If there are no witnesses to confirm the father's suspicions, he merely gives the child a warning. When asked whether a child is punished for lying, many Sisala reply that a "small boy" always tells lies because he fears what his father will do to him if he tells the truth. Although a child is punished for being disrespectful of people and property, his behavior as a "small boy" along with its negative aspects, such as lying, is reinforced in his proper relationship to authority.

The second concept which can be translated as "respect" is that of *zile* or "respectful politeness." The Sisala often say, "We respect (*zile*) our brothers, but we give both fear (*fa*) and respect (*zile*) to our fathers." Whereas *fa* expresses a "one-way" kind of respect, that of *zile* is largely reciprocal. A younger brother is expected to show respect to his elder brother; and conversely, the elder brother is to give courtesy to his younger sibling. In sum, *zile* refers to the polite respect stemming from a person's awareness of another's position whether he be stranger (*nihuoro*), friend (*nadongngo*), or elder (*nihiang*). A boy begins to learn the rules of politeness at about six years of age when he is expected to give a brief greeting (*lollung*) and acknowledge the presence of others about him, but the notion becomes most important when he reaches adolescence. As the child learns *zile,* he is learning the proper manner in which to relate to people who occupy different social positions.

The concepts of *fa* and *zile* are also related to the child's respect for property or "things" (*kia*). When a child is taught to respect "things," he is being taught to respect the "owner of things" (*kiatina*) and in turn the owner's rights in things. Sisala parents often remark that small children are usually able to recognize the ownership of various objects in the house, and the child himself is regarded as *tina* or "owner" of his own toys and other possessions. This concept of ownership applies not only to things but also to people who occupy positions of authority: headman of the *janwuo* or "house owner" (*diatina*), person who performs sacrifices or "shrine owner" (*venetina*), and medicine man or "medicine owner" (*dalusuntina*). The child must learn to relate to persons in positions of authority and to show them fear and respect; he is expected to attach similar values to objects symbolic of this authority.

Acts of disrespect for property connected with authority are regarded as severe transgressions and often as taboos. This is especially true for the elder children in the *janwuo* who are viewed as the potential inheritors of the family wealth; thus an "eldest son" is enjoined from handling or using such articles as his father's clothing and ritual objects. In some cases the violation of these norms places the individual in a state of ritual danger as, for example, were an elder son to reach into his father's granary (*vire*). Thus, property taboos function to protect the father's exclusive rights in the property.

A man in his capacity as "owner" is also perceived as a provider and protector. During his early years the child comes to see his father (or father's brothers) as the source of protection against the often dangerous and unpredictable world about him. When he is sick, it is the "owner of medicines" who provides the means for his recovery. As he grows older, he comes to see that it is the head of the compound (*baviretina* or "owner of the large granary") and his younger brothers (*viretinaba* or "owners of the small granaries") who provide the foodstuffs for the women in the house. He also sees that his mother must ask or "beg" the father for the millet and other foodstuffs with which to prepare her meals. The learning of "respect," therefore, involves the child's recognition of his father's position as protector and provider. If a boy wants money for a cloth, he must "beg" his father. Until recent times it was unheard of for a boy to earn his own money and keep it for his private use; rather, he was supposed to give it to his father or to the *diatina* as a "kindness," and if at a later time he wanted something, he had to "beg" his father.

Sisala parents never use deprivation as a form of punishment, for it is believed that if a father deprives his son of food, the son will come to "hate" the father and will beg food from strangers, thereby insulting his family. If a father refuses his son, the boy will lose respect for him and the boy's friends will ridicule him saying that he has a poor family. It is believed that a child who is well fed and clothed will respect his father and act in proper ways.

The following two accounts of memorable childhood experiences point out the child's perception of his father as a nurturant protector. The first describes a child's reaction to the death of his father:

> I was ten years old and my father was in Kumasi. I returned one evening from the bush with my brothers, when my father (father's brother) called me. When I stepped into his room, he said, "Prepare for Kumasi" in a screaming voice. To these words I was astonished. He said again, "Prepare for Kumasi, your father is dead." He did not complete the word "dead" when tears started to pierce through my eyes and run to my chin . . . After the funeral, I packed my luggage and returned to Tumu. I was not happy at all. In fact, I had the idea that I wouldn't be able to finish my studies, because my backbone was broken and I had no helper to encourage me to go to school.

The second account involves a child who witnessed his father's millet crop destroyed by fire. Note how the boy shares his father's sorrow and how he learns from this the importance of social responsibility:

> I can remember when my father's millet burned and I was informed. I was first weeping like a "small boy" for food when my elder brother came. When he told me that my father's millet field was burning, I became very quiet and listened keenly to what he said. I was only six years old then. I followed my brother to the farm. I saw the millet burning and I wept bitterly . . . The following day we went and gathered the millet that wasn't burned. The millet was kept in baskets that numbered only 25. However, this didn't last us, and my father had to sell a cow to buy food. This taught me not to be a "small boy" and always cry about food. In fact, the day the millet burned, I was very sorry and I didn't eat. So I learned from that day that I must always go to the farm and watch the millet. Because I always think that our millet might burn again, and so I am always there to protect the millet from cows and also from burning. Even still, when my father thinks of that year, he becomes very sad.

Most parents readily admit that their children are well behaved and respectful to all of their elders. When asked why, they often say that a child learns to fear both his father and his father's brothers and that in fact the father's brother is more strict since his brother's children are not of his own blood. If a child violates a moral custom or causes economic damage to his family, it is often the father's brother who punishes the child. Were the father to intervene, he would be committing a violation of ancestral custom by denying his brother rights over his own children. In effect, the Sisala say that a child learns to fear all of his fathers (*nyimmaba*) and he knows he cannot hide from them. Though parents speak from time to time of the need of "beating their children properly," I never saw a single case of corporal punishment. For the most part, punishments consisted of threats or shouts of anger.

Respect for male authority is, in the last analysis, absolute. The child learns respect not only in terms of his father and father's brothers but also in reference to all males of the ascending generation. The Sisala have a proverb which states, "If you give birth to a child, it belongs to everyone" (*ng ni lul bie nu kalal kung ne*), and this means that the behavior and welfare of any child is the responsibility of all people. If a boy misbehaves in a public place, any older man can take the boy in charge and report the case to his father. Conversely, if a father is seen beating his child with undue severity, any stranger may approach the father and "beg" him to stop, in which case the father would have to stop or else he would insult the stranger. In the child's eye, then, the unity of male authority within the *janwuo* expressed in the reciprocal rights of the father and father's brother with each other's children is transferred to all males of the ascending generation.

In contrast to the boy's relationship with the father and other figures of male authority, the relationship with his mother always remains relatively warm and free. As a child he often asks his mother to buy him gifts in the marketplace; as he grows older, he is expected to reciprocate by helping her with her garden or by buying her a cloth. When he reaches the age of six, however, he learns that "sense" is a quality to be acquired from his father. The mother is supposed to help in this realization by encouraging her son to associate with his father, and if a child fails to make such an identification, the fault is often attributed to the mother for wanting to possess her boy and for not allowing him to become a man. By the age of six or seven the boy has moved out of his mother's room and lives and eats with his brothers or fathers.

A Sisala girl is not subject to the same kind of authoritarian relationships as the boy. When she reaches the age of seven years, she has very little association with her real father or father's brothers. Fathers often say that when a girl reaches this age, she should be learning the "ways of women," and that such womanly things are not the concern of men. Except for moral questions involving the welfare and integrity of the *janwuo*, the responsibility for the daughter's training is left solely to the mother and the mother's co-wives (who are often the mother's sisters). In contrast with the father-son relationship, a girl's relationship with her mother is warm and affectionate. Since her older sisters are frequently married and living in other villages, the daughter spends a large part of the time helping her mother. Mothers regard daughters as great comforts and as persons with whom they can talk freely about the everyday problems of the house. As the girl grows older and is more able to share the household tasks, the mother-daughter relationship becomes more intense, largely because of the realization that it will soon be partially broken by the daughter's marriage. The strength of this relationship is often expressed in times of crisis, such as divorce when the Sisala remark that a boy usually sides with his father while a girl cries bitterly at the loss of her mother.

The preceding discussion of the educational process has been viewed primarily from the perspective of the parental generation. At this point the subject must be examined from the viewpoint of the growing child, particularly the dynamics of sibling unity and conflict, and the child's reaction to male parental authority.

In interviews children often express resentment at having been exploited by their elder brothers, recalling malicious acts done to them when they were unable to defend themselves. The following statement is typical:

> When I was a child, my older brother was a bad boy. Often my mother asked him to take care of me when she went away for a short time. My brother would then take me out, and when he saw my mother coming from the river where she had gone to draw water, my brother would pinch me with his fingernails. I would cry, and my mother would come for me and collect me. My brother would then go and play.

Children also recall times when their brothers refused to play or else gave them inferior roles in their games. Teasing by older brothers is very common; the younger sibling is taunted as "small boy" who sleeps with his mother or who is always dirty because he is unable to wash himself. Other notions attached to the term "small boy" include: always annoys his mother and father, cries when his mother is gone, thinks only of food, does not work and never stops playing, does not understand his father's warnings, and does not know enough to fear God.

The effect of this experience intensifies the child's desire to grow up and to achieve a position where he will no longer be dominated by his older brothers. Although some people express a certain nostalgia for the carefree ways of childhood, the idea of being like a child again is regarded by most Sisala as utter foolishness: only a "useless" person would want to be like a "small boy." Therefore, as the child reaches the age of six years, the previous notion of the "helpless infant" now becomes that of the "useless child" or "small boy," and as the child becomes aware of this negative image of himself, he is strongly motivated to grow up.

The following statement exemplifies this desire to grow up.

> A Sisala man does not like to talk about the future or else he will become jealous. Also we don't like to talk about things in the past. There are some people who act like children, but they are fools and useless people. When I was young, I was a junior and was abused by elder people. Now I am older and I don't have to take such nonsense. All children want to grow up so they can be equal with others. We have a proverb: "*la mu sia ne, la bi hari mu*" or "forwards ever, backwards never." It is foolish to think of being a child again.

In contrast to the younger child's perception and reaction to his elder brother, older Sisala children never admit to purposely harming a younger brother or having feelings of malice and jealousy. The older sibling says that his younger brother is helpless and without "sense" and therefore must be protected and taught. The following statement is typical of the strained patience and attitude of parental protectiveness assumed by the elder sibling:

> When my brother was two years old, I used to take care of him for my mother. With this boy, if I did something wrong, my father would beat me. I remember one time he fell down and he had one of his teeth broken and lost some blood. I felt very sad that day for my brother. When my father came home, he beat me properly, and so I felt very sorry myself also. . . . One day when I took him outside to give my mother a rest, he shit on me and on my clothes. I was very sorry for myself that morning. But I was also happy because my father was there when this thing happened.

Although aggressive or hostile feelings exist, they are obviously suppressed by the fear of parental punishment and the assumption of a parental protective role.

In sum, the parental norm stressing sibling unity and the reality of conflict together create an important dynamic principle governing the growth process among Sisala children. While the child is supposed to accept the submissive and obedient role of a younger brother, he is actually motivated to reject his "small boy" status and to strive to attain equality with his elder brothers. The tendencies which create conflict in the elder brother-younger brother relationship also serve the parental value of sibling unity by promoting eventual sibling equality at adolescence. The child in his role as elder brother, on the other hand, is not supposed to demonstrate any aggressive behavior toward his younger sibling even though such behavior might seem justified in light of the favoritism shown the younger child. Instead, these aggressive tendencies are culturally channeled into the authoritarian role which the elder sibling is expected to accept. As the child matures into adulthood the semiauthoritarian role of the elder brother provides the model from which develops the fully authoritarian role of the father. Thus, the prestige or status connected with the role of protector-disciplinarian serves to compensate for the suppression of aggressive behavior.

The child's perception of the authority of the ascending male generation appears to be absolute. Whereas he sees his mother and women in general to be flexible, inconsistent, and capable of being manipulated, he views his father and father's brothers as presenting a united front, impervious to the sentimental weaknesses of women. This fear of paternal authority is demonstrated in childhood recollections concerning acts of thievery. In no cases did children mention stealing from their fathers or other lineally related male adults; most of the incidents involved stealing from strangers (most commonly market women) or taking food while their mothers were cooking. Most children feel they could either bluff their mothers or prevent them from reporting the incident to their fathers. Punishment administered by one's father is seen as a fearful occasion, and most children mentioned their desire to run away when directly confronted by their fathers, while at the same time pointing out the futility of trying to escape their fathers' anger.

The following episode related by a child clearly points up the unified and absolute nature of parental authority while the involvement of the police provides an interesting extension to the principles of male authority.

> I and my friends went to a valley near Tumu to steal some mangoes. Nobody else was near. We went into the garden but left one person outside to watch to see if anybody was coming. But he ran away when he saw the owner of the trees coming and he didn't warn us. So the owner came quietly into the garden and suddenly grabbed me. My other friends ran away. The owner gave me two slaps on the face. People began gathering around and they were hooting at me and telling the owner to beat me harder. Afterwards they brought me to my father, and he beat me very well. My father then took me to the police station and told the policeman to beat me also. I was put in jail for two days; I was very frightened and so you see I will never forget this. I was seven years old at the time. Now I am older and I have learned that stealing is wrong.

While fear is the main reaction to parental authority, the virtue of cleverness is also important. Parents see cleverness in the child's astute perception of parental wishes, but children view cleverness in terms of their ability to manipulate people in authority and thereby avoid punishment. This notion of cleverness finds an interesting parallel in the behavior of the "trickster" of Sisala folktales. In these tales the trickster, whether he be spider, rabbit, or monkey, is characteristically small, somewhat ludicrous, foolish in deportment, but extremely clever. His adversaries include both the larger animals such as elephant and lion and human figures of authority such as headmen and chiefs. Although these adversaries are seen as possessing power either by virtue of their size and strength or by virtue of their status in the society, they are also viewed as capable of being fooled. In a typical story involving human authority figures, the chief presents a difficult problem to his people, makes a wager, or else holds a contest. The trickster answers the challenge and proceeds to solve the problem or win the contest through cleverly devious means. In so doing he often implicates the chief or else makes him look foolish. The cleverness of the trickster, therefore, consists of his ability to manipulate people in authority and to evade punishment. In no cases does he ever commit an act of disrespect or directly confront or challenge the figure of power and authority.

Differential interpretations are given folktales by parents and children. Parents state that they tell tales to children because they enjoy entertaining their children and because the tales teach them moral lessons. Tales often end in a "riddle" in which the main character is presented with a dilemma involving a series of choices or courses of action. Children are then tested by having to make a choice which in turn involves the learning of a moral lesson.

Children, on the other hand, often omit the moral lessons when relating tales, stressing instead the plot and social interaction of the characters; it is the cleverness of the trickster which is foremost in their minds. In nontrickster tales, usually consisting of epic adventures or hearsay experiences of others, children often place themselves and their friends in the roles of the main characters. Although they admit that such tales are make-believe, the involvement they demonstrate in identifying with the characters shows the degree to which they identify with the virtue of cleverness which the characters exhibit.

Sisala children show an astute perception of the nature of adult authority and for evaluating the consequences of their actions in terms of the particular configuration of authority with which they must interact. If a group of boys plans to steal something, the nature of their opponent is analyzed at great length. Children are also very good mimics of the speech and actions of others, especially of those in positions of authority. These imitations are often derogatory, emphasizing physical imperfections, speech impediments, and foolishness of demeanor. While this kind of mimicry provides a passive outlet for aggressive feelings, it also reflects understanding of authority figures, and this is used by children to manipulate their parents and thereby achieve a favorable position. This is reflected in the following childhood recollection.

> One of our father's brothers used to beat the children in the house with little or no provocation. One day, when we were children, we were bringing the sheep in from the fields. One of the sheep was missing. This man then yelled at us, and said that if we did not find the lost sheep, we would not have any food and water. Then he began chasing the children around the compound. But we were smart. We ran over to where our father was sitting. Our father's brother didn't see this, and when he caught one of the children, he began beating the boy properly. Our father saw this and he came down. He went up to the man and told him to release the child, saying that one sheep doesn't make any difference, and that the children were hungry and could not be denied food. We children were all giggling to ourselves, saying, "Good, good, for our father."

We have seen that as the child approaches the age of six years, he begins to perceive himself in the negative image of the "small boy." This image is created and reinforced by the teasing and ridicule of elder siblings and by parental expectations. As the child internalizes this image, he is also motivated to change it, patterning himself on the role model of his elder brother. The father and other adult males are perceived as somewhat distant, and their authority is considered absolute. Although the child expresses positive sentiments for the nurturant and protective aspects of his father's roles, he fears his father and father's brothers and tries to avoid any action or situation which might produce punishment or public shame. On the other hand, the rather wretched self-image of the "small boy" is compensated for by the somewhat covetous identification with the virtue of "cleverness" exemplified in the various "trickster" heroes of folktales.

ADOLESCENCE TO MANHOOD: TEN TO FIFTEEN YEARS

When a boy reaches the age of ten, he is called *bapuasi* or "getting on to manhood," and he is expected to begin to acquire the "sense" of a man.

This means he should not only know the difference between right and wrong, but also act in proper ways without parental supervision. As he demonstrates this and as he begins taking greater interest in the activities of his fathers, he is assigned greater responsibility. He is now fully responsible for the grazing of animals and the education of his younger brothers. On the farm he is given the job of planting and is allowed to help his fathers with the weeding and harvesting of the crops. A girl of this age, called *hatolo* or "young woman," learns to prepare meals and develops an independent interest in household work. By the age of twelve or thirteen she is entrusted with all the domestic duties her mother would perform and is often sent to market to buy and sell.

Between the ages of ten and twelve a boy disassociates himself from imaginative childhood play and forms a deeper and more mature association with his fathers. Indicative of this change is his manner of deportment and mastery of etiquette. When a boy meets any senior male, he is expected to kneel before him, shake his hand, and offer a greeting (*lollung*), consisting of the initial statement, *n dia pina,* or "How is your day?" to which the elder replies, *o wering* or "It is fine." These reciprocal transactions are repeated seven to ten more times, during which the junior person inquires about such things as the man's state of health, his wife and children, or current events. To extend a greeting from a distance or to assume any other position than kneeling would be considered gross impropriety and disrespect for age.

As the boy develops into manhood, he is subject to different kinds of discipline from those he endured as a child. When referring to the adolescent, the Sisala often say, "When a stick is wet, bend it; because when it is dry, it will break," indicating that a child who is not trained properly when young cannot be disciplined when older. The physical punishment of childhood is replaced by verbal abuse, and feelings of shame take precedence over those of fear. If a young man refuses to go to the farm, the other people in the house, including children, ridicule him by calling him a "useless boy" (*bichuola*), and if the boy does not repair his ways, he is warned that no prospective father-in-law will allow him to marry his daughter.

In the event that an older boy commits a gross act of disrespect, the father may swear (*kabre*) upon him a curse by the ancestors. This is done by the father pounding his fist on the ground and saying, "You (the ancestors), I have never done such a thing to you. I don't know about this boy." The mother's curse is also regarded as a very serious matter; if the son has a serious quarrel with his mother, she may reply, "If I am not the person who brought you forth in blood and suffered so many things with you, you may do as you like. But if I am, you will not see tomorrow's sunset." In both cases it is believed that the boy will die, and often a curse creates such a state of despondency in the young man that he will commit suicide rather than await the wrath of the ancestors. Most of the cases of suicide which I have recorded resulted from such curses.

The acquisition of increased responsibility also affects the boy's relationships with elder siblings. Since the young man is no longer required to be submissive to and dependent upon his elder brother, the relationship is transformed into one based upon equality and mutual respect. The teacher-learner relationship now becomes one of co-workers united in a common economic pursuit with each party respecting the rights and opinions of the other. Several Sisala proverbs (*namaka*) express this emerging principle of reciprocity. "When I fall and you fall, it is fair play" (*tel dintel ninga gbele*); this means that each party in a relationship must contribute an equal share to its maintenance. If two brothers develop a heated argument, one may say, "If you hold and I hold too tightly, it will break the calabash" (*keng di mi keng kiase gbanga*). Proverbs such as these are often used as subtle means of social control when the sibling relationship is threatened by divisive behavior.

One effect of the norm of reciprocity is to increase the feeling of unity among siblings within the *janwuo*. It will be recalled that parental emphasis on sibling solidarity is begun in childhood. This is often done by creating feelings of suspicion and hostility toward people living in other compounds. Parents tell their children not to wander in the village or accept food from strangers, warning them that there are "evil people" and "witches" who might poison them. Parents also bring children into their petty quarrels with other compounds in the village. One Sisala man related to me one such typical quarrel he remembers from his childhood.

> When I was a child, we lived in the upper compounds. The people of the lower compounds tabooed "hot porridge" (*kulung*). That is, they always ate hot porridge but they tabooed the word, especially around dinner time. One of the women in my compound, when she prepared her meal, would always yell "*kulung*" when her meal was ready. However, she always yelled this loud enough so that people of the lower compounds could hear. When they heard it, they had to go hungry that night because they couldn't eat their *kulung*. We children used to think it was very funny and used to join in. One day an elder man from the lower compounds came and accused my father's people of doing this. But my father bluffed the man saying he knew nothing about it. The man was very angry when he went away, and all of us children laughed very hard. This is one reason why we aren't very friendly with the people of the lower compounds.

This essentially negative approach to sibling solidarity takes on a more positive aspect during adolescence. A boy speaks of "talking deeply" with his brothers and confiding problems and secrets which he would not share with another. Concerning the loyalty among brothers, the Sisala often quote the proverb: "The cockroach said: To throw your friend before a hen is no joke" (*loriming ni bula jung dong a lo jiming sipang na bi gbele nga*). Whereas a younger child would report the misdeeds of his brother to his father, the adolescent feels a greater loyalty to his brother.

Changes in play and recreational activities also mark early adolescence. Previous play activities stressed the theme of sociability and a degree of role differentiation between the elder and younger siblings; now the emphasis is friendly competition and an equality of roles. Some of the more common pastimes are wrestling, target shooting with bows and arrows, and a game resembling field hockey called *kpabing*. The betting of cowrie shells and pennies often adds to the excitement of these contests. All these games are tests of skill and strength, and the winner of the contest carries an informal title of achievement among his "brothers" and age mates.

Principles of equality and reciprocity are also reflected in a boy's relationships with age mates and friends. Prior to the age of ten the "social space" of the child is confined essentially to the minor lineage settlement. Although he travels outside of this area from time to time, it is always in the presence of an older sibling or adult. With the increased responsibilities of early adolescence, the boy is allowed to move freely within the village and to travel to other villages unaccompanied by adults, and this leads to the formation of relationships beyond the immediate kin group. The Sisala word for "friend," *nadongngo* (literally, "person each other"), connotes the ideas of equality, reciprocity, and mutual aid. A young man's relationships with his friends, however, do not exhibit the same solidarity as those with his brother. Although he would not betray the confidences of a friend, neither would he confide deep problems and secrets involving personal and family matters. The interaction among friends and age mates is generally free and not deeply involved with personal matters.

As the boy reaches adulthood, interests begun in childhood mature into definite occupational and role specializations. In addition to farming and herding, every Sisala man possesses at least one specialization. Male avocations include weaving, sewing, leatherwork, weapon making, hunting, blacksmithing, xylophone playing, praise singing, and divining. The development of these skills is determined by parental encouragement of the perceived interests of the child. Thus, if a boy's father or father's brother is a blacksmith and if the boy is always in the company of this man and expresses an interest in blacksmithing, he is encouraged to participate. In the case of the "eldest son" (*bihiang*) the direction of certain interests is predetermined; because he is the potential inheritor of the *janwuo* and the office of *diatina*, special concern is given to his learning of the family traditions. Because of the taboos inherent in his relationship with his biological father, his grandfather or another male elder of the house is entrusted with his education.

Certain male specializations are connected with a group of spiritual entities called *tome*. These include hunting, *tome;* blacksmithing, *lukuru tome;* xylophone playing, *luri tome;* praise singing, *goka tome;* and divining, *vuruga tome*. Each of these *tome* has a shrine within the *janwuo*. It is believed that sometime during late childhood or adolescence a *tome* may come down and "reincarnate" or "marry" the boy. When this happens, the boy exhibits strange behavior, and a diviner is consulted to ascertain whether he has been "reincarnated." If this is the case, sacrifices are performed to the *tome,* and henceforth the boy is expected to follow the will of the *tome* and pursue his particular specialization.

Although a boy may be reincarnated by a *tome* at birth, it is the "secondary reincarnation" or "marriage" with the *tome* during adolescence which figures most significantly in the determination of his eventual specialization. It is also believed that the *tome* only enters a child who has shown a previous interest in the specialization, and this combination of factors is demonstrated in the following statements. The first relates how one Sisala man became a xylophone player.

> When I was a young boy about eight years old, I used to get up and always be playing my father's xylophone with my hands. At funerals, I would always be sitting by my father and watching him play. When my father would stop playing, I would again be playing the xylophone with my hands. When I was about ten or twelve years old, I became very sick. I slept often and was too weak to lift my hands and legs. So my father consulted a diviner, and the diviner said that the *luri tome* had entered me. My father then returned and sacrificed to the *luri*, saying, "If you are the *tome* which comes to my child, then let him become a good xylophone player." My father then gave me a set of xylophone sticks, and in a few days I was feeling better. I learned to play the xylophone pretty much by myself. I would also sit with my father and watch him play and imitate what he did. It did not take me long to learn how to play—only three years—because the *luri* guided me. When I was young like this, I would watch my father sacrifice to the *luri*, and he would give me herbs so I could play better.

A second statement relates how a Sisala man became a diviner or *vuruga*. Note in this case the informant had no prior inclination toward divining.

> I grew up to the age of twenty years. Then suddenly I became very ill; my mind was mixed up and I was saying strange things to other people. I almost died. And so my father got up and went to a diviner. Here my father was told that I was going to be a *vuruga*, for the *vuruga tome* had entered me. My father then cut a stick from a certain tree and assembled the elder men of the house. While I wasn't looking, they buried some cowrie shells outside. Then they sacrificed some fowls to the *vuruga tome* and buried their heads and feet outside. I didn't see where any of these things were buried. One of the old men of the house held the top of the stick and I held the bottom part of it. The elder man then asked me to locate where these things were buried. So we went around and I found the things one by one. If I would have missed one, I wouldn't have become a good *vuruga*.

The undertaking of a particular specialization involves a special relationship to the spirit or *tome* responsible for the person's newly acquired talent. A young man who becomes a blacksmith has the responsibility to care for and observe the taboos related to the "blacksmith spirit" (*lukuru tome*) and the various related medicines (*dalusun*). If he has trouble in his work, if his ironwork cracks or breaks after cooling, it may mean that he has broken a certain taboo or his *tome* is "thirsty" and its shrine needs to be sacrificed. If a more senior blacksmith is persent in the *janwuo*, the young man only observes or assists in the sacrifices, but if he is the only blacksmith, the "ownership" of the *tome* and related medicines would be his. This basic pattern holds true for all the *tome*-related specializations.

The Sisala's perception of the learning process inherent in *tome*-related specializations deserves special comment. Whereas farming and other forms of work are essentially group enterprises learned through observation and imitation, the *tome*-related specializations are individual pursuits in which the acquisition of appropriate skills is largely determined by supernatural forces. With the exception of hunting, and to a lesser degree xylophone playing, one's talent or skill in a particular avocation is directly attributed to the strength of the related *tome*. In considering the Sisala belief in the nature of the learning process, it may be seen that little value is attached to individual achievement and initiative. A child learns to be a good farmer because he is respectful and obedient toward his father and elder brothers, and he becomes a good specialist because he is respectful and obedient to his *tome* and to the overall supernatural order.

While the Sisala place little value on individual autonomy, the period of adolescence does allow for a certain expression of independence, primarily of an economic nature. By the time a boy reaches the age of twelve or thirteen, he has sufficiently mastered the skills of farming to establish his private plot. While his primary obligation lies with the family farm, free time may be spent cultivating his own farm which is usually located within the village. With the exception of millet, the main dietary staple, he is allowed to grow all other crops and to market them. With the proceeds he may buy an item of clothing or small livestock such as fowl and goats. The Sisala often comment that a boy's desire in learning to farm is related to his desire to be an "owner of things" (*kiatina*); they say that a "small boy" has nothing and must cry and beg, whereas a young man has money and can buy drinks for his friends.

This growing economic independence creates tensions in the father-son relationship. While the young man has a strong tendency to acquire property or "things" like his father, in order to gain a degree of personal prestige as an "owner" and to maintain the reciprocal obligations of his friendships, he is also expected to offer his earnings to his father as a "kindness" or act of respect. The Sisala say, however, that if a man is wealthy, he would never accept his son's earnings, although he would expect him to make the offer as a sign of respect. As long as the father is wealthy, or at least behaves in the manner of a wealthy man (*kuoro*), the father-son relationship is usually amicable and stable. If the father is poor, however, and demands the earnings of his sons, he not only deprives his sons of their private wealth but also comes to occupy a position of low status and respect since he is apparently no longer able to nurture and protect his family. When the Sisala say, "Poor person has no friends" (*summo bi nandong kene*), they mean that a man without wealth is unable to provide for his family or to maintain his friendships. In the last analysis, to be "poor" often means to be "bad" (*bong*), for the wealth of a house depends upon both the strength of the ancestors and minor deities and the goodness of its people.

The problem of personal versus family wealth must also be seen in terms of the larger question of family prestige. The Sisala have a proverb which states, "If you aren't there, I am not there." In the context of the family this means that if a young man's father is poor, the young man can be nothing else but poor. In the traditional setting the very thought of a young man striving to attain independent wealth is unheard of, if not irrational. As the boy approaches manhood, he comes to see that his own identity is directly related to that of his family, clan section, and village. And with the increased responsibilities of age he seeks through his work to enhance the prestige of his family. Thus, many Sisala men express great personal pride at having bought a cow for their fathers (in this case, the *diatina*) with money they had saved. Since cattle are regarded as the highest index of wealth, the gift of a cow to add to the family herd is seen as a supreme act of love for one's family.

The internalization of "sense" during adolescence is directly related to the young man's perception of himself in terms of his family. Whereas a child is taught proper behavior through fear of his father, a young man, who has already acquired "sense," is expected to feel shame if he acts in an improper manner. If a young man steals another's property or commits an act of gross disrespect, his actions reflect upon his family's name, for the whole family collectively endures the shame incurred by one of its members. Thus, not only does the individual suffer shame in a personal sense, but he also experiences a loss in his self-image as a result of the ridicule his family must suffer.

This internalization of the moral prescriptions of Sisala culture in terms of family identity also makes the young man an effective agent of social control, for he sees himself as not only obeying his father's teachings but also as actively maintaining his family's prestige. While not yet able to participate in the council of his elders, he does take part in "family discussions" with his brothers in which problems are discussed and quarrels or misunderstandings which might threaten the unity of the family are resolved. These private and confidential sessions may be seen as miniature versions of those meetings conducted by the elder generation and they serve to provide practice for the time when the younger men will inherit the *janwuo*.

On occasion members of the younger generation may even protest the actions of their fathers as threatening the unity or prestige of the family. The following statement relates one such incident:

> My father is a very wealthy man. He has so many cattle that when the tax people come to count them—well, the whole herd can fill the village. He is also a generous man. Some people, you know, are wealthy but they are selfish. We fear such people, but we don't respect them. My father is both very wealthy and very generous. One time, however, he saw that the chief of Tumu had a lorry [i.e., truck] and so he wanted one too. I became very angry and I told my father that a lorry would bring him a large debt but that cattle would never give a man a debt. I even threatened to leave him and go to Kumasi. But my father is a very wise man. He understood and he didn't by it. I feared that my father would become poor, and then where would I be? For, we Sisala say, "If you aren't there, I am not there." For if the father is nobody, then the son is nobody.

The transition from the status of "young man" (*bapuasi*) or "young woman" (*hatolo*) to that of "man" (*baala*) or "woman" (*haala*) is not marked by ceremonies of initiation or puberty. This may be explained by the

Older girls pound yams for the evening meal.

fact that no aspect of adult culture and behavior, except sexual intercourse, is denied to the child's awareness. Thus, the need to educate the child into the secrets of the adult world is lacking. A second and perhaps even more important reason lies in the sociopsychological dynamics of the growth process itself. The six-year-old exhibits a strong desire to grow up, and parents, instead of discouraging this tendency, encourage the child's development of responsibility within the limits of his perceived capacity. The boy, therefore, voluntarily breaks the affective-indulgent tie with his mother and begins striving at a young age to achieve adult responsibility and status. The transition from childhood to adulthood, then, is a gradual process characterized by an assumption of increased responsibilities, a greater pursuit of individual interests, and an increasing identification with one's family.

3/Adult culture and personality

AGE: PROPERTY, AUTHORITY, AND THE POSITION OF WOMEN

When a boy reaches the age of fifteen, he is considered a man (*baala*) and is expected to perform adult labor and to have the requisite sexual prowess necessary for marriage. Sexual expression and play before manhood is viewed by the Sisala as a serious moral offense and punishment is severe. Since sexual intercourse is viewed as a "powerful" activity requiring the maturity of age, the Sisala believe that the commission of a sexual act during childhood or adolescence causes a boy to become weak and impotent and a girl to become barren and lazy. Almost any sexual relationship between a boy and a girl is incestuous since most of the child's relationships exist within the context of the minor lineage settlement. Incest is considered a violation of ancestral custom which endangers not only the life of the parties involved but also the welfare of the entire *janwuo* (patrilocal extended family).

Between the ages of fifteen and eighteen a young man spends much time in association with his age mates, attending public occasions such as funerals and markets. In this setting he begins to contract relationships with young women from other villages. While the Sisala disapprove of premarital sexual unions, such behavior is nonetheless expected of young men and women, and virginity is not seen as a prerequisite for marriage. For the most part, such sexual unions lead to courtship and eventually marriage, especially if the woman conceives.

Marriage among the Sisala is more than a husband-wife relationship; it is also a contractual relationship between two groups, the one which "gives away (a daughter) in marriage" (*buge*) and the one which "collects or marries (a wife)" (*ja*). A young man desiring to enter into marriage is always supported by the older male members of his house. When he goes to his future wife's people to announce his intentions, the various "courting gifts" are supplied by the *diatina* (owner) of his house, and he is always accompanied by an older brother or father. The idea of entering into a marital contract alone is impossible since a young man could not supply the cow needed for the "bride price" (*jaarang*). The wife's parents are concerned about not only the prospective husband but also the family into which their daughter will marry. Once the marital union is established, both families have a vested concern in the stability of the marriage. In the event of a divorce the relationship and prestige of the two families are threatened. If the wife returns to her own family, her fathers insist she go back to her husband; if she adamantly refuses, the wife's family attempts to find another wife for the husband in order to repair the relationship. To return the bride price means to sever the relationship and to deprive the husband's family of a source of childbearing.

With marriage comes the final establishment of the young man's adult status. When one Sisala man was asked why people marry, he replied with astonishment, "Why do I farm? Because if I didn't, I would have nothing to feed my family. Why should I marry? Because if I didn't, I would have no family to feed." This statement typifies the notion that marriage is one of the unquestioned necessities of life and that the purpose of marriage is to have children over whom the father assumes a nurturant and protective role. The assumption of the role of father represents a culmination of behavior patterns and values learned as a child, for it is based upon the child's strong identification with paternal male authority and his exercise of these nurturant and protective qualities in the semiauthoritarian role as an elder brother.

A man marries at about the age of eighteen, and soon after, if fortunate, he becomes a father. However, until about the age of thirty he is still subject to the authority of his father and father's brothers, and this is a period of growing intergenerational conflict. The young man's authority over his wife and children is not yet complete, for he still must "beg" from his father the basic necessities of every day subsistence. Even though he is now allowed to participate in discussions of family affairs, he must always defer to the decisions of his elders. And since the *janwuo* is large and since the inheritance of family property and succession to authority passes to the next younger brother, a young man does not attain full rights of authority until the last member of his father's generation dies.

The ceremonial practices involved in inheritance and succession within the *janwuo* may be viewed as a belated "rite of passage" in which the younger generation of brothers and cousins collectively assume the real authority in the family. With the death of the last member of the senior generation the office of *diatina* passes to the "eldest son" (*bihiang*) or the eldest member of the junior generation. The "eldest son" then performs a series of sacrifices called *bille nasing* or "washing away the hand" from the family possessions and shrines. Since as an "eldest son" he was not allowed to handle the possessions of his fathers while they were living, he says when performing sacrifices, "When my father was alive, I obeyed the custom. Now he is dead, and I go against it." By this kind of process all of the family property, shrines, and medicines are transferred to the new "house owner." However, the Sisala readily point out that the family property is never shared among brothers but is collectively inherited with the *diatina* occupying a position of first among equals. Thus, the succession of the "eldest son" to the office of *diatina* means, in effect, the succession of all his brothers to a similar position of authority in the *janwuo*.

A close relationship exists among age, property, and authority. When a young boy is taught to respect his father and to defer to the wisdom of his age, this includes respect for the father's property and his right to control it. In the context of the *janwuo* the *diatina* or "house owner" is the one who exercises control over all the family property. He "owns" the main granary (*bavire*) from which he redistributes millet to the respective nuclear family units in the *janwuo* and he "owns" the family cattle and sheep which are used for sacrifices and bride wealth payments. A person who is a *tina* (owner)—whether he be *diatina, dalusuntina* ("medicine owner"), or *venetina* ("shrine owner")—does not have the right to alienate his property, and thus the term *tina* may best be translated as "custodian." When a man inherits the family property, he inherits the right and responsibility to direct its use in the interest of the whole family. The Sisala would say that the houses they live in and the land they farm "belong" to the ancestors, and that they have been given to the present generation of "owners" (*tinaba*) as a sacred trust to be used wisely and to be passed on to the next generation.

The effect of European contact has introduced new variables into the nature of political authority, but the principle of seniority remains basic to the understanding of the political process in Sisala society. When the heads of the various extended families of the clan section meet to discuss their common problems, the most senior *diatina* of those assembled assumes the position of first among equals. If the *diatina* of one *janwuo* is a member of the junior generation, he has little or no power to affect the decisions of his elder men in the affairs of the clan section. The same holds true in the affairs of the village. Since the office of chieftain is passed on from father to son and usually remains in the same family, it often happens that the chief (*kuoro*) is younger than the elder men in his village. In this case the office of chieftain and that of the *diatina* are separate, and while the chief may represent his village in certain political affairs, he has no power over the wealth and property of his own house. Unless he aspires to purely personal political ambitions, the power of his office lies with the elder men of the various compounds of the village.

The traditional values attached to age and authority are more clearly reflected in the ritual authority of the *jangtina* or "village owner" than in the secular authority of the village chief. Unlike chieftaincy, the office of *jangtina* is succeeded to by the next oldest member of the appropriate lineage. Whereas each of the "house owners" represents the secular authority of their respective household units, the *jangtina*, who may also be a *diatina* in his own house, is the ritual authority and custodian of the village. His main duty consists of sacrificing to the village shrine (*vene*). During times of warfare and intravillage conflict, or periodically prior to the planting of crops, the *jangtina* sacrifices to the village shrine in order to secure the protection of the gods (*vesing*), to promote the fertility of the land, and to repair serious disputes within the village. Since the *jangtina* comes from that lineage or clan section which was thought to have settled the area first, the village shrine of which he is the "owner" is believed to be ancestral and therefore more powerful than the shrines of the particular extended families and clan sections. Even though he does not act upon matters affecting the village without the consent of the village elders, his position as first among equals stems largely from his affiliation with and custodianship of the village shrine.

When a man reaches the age of about fifty, he achieves the status of "elder man" (*banihiang*), and he assumes a position of greater authority in village affairs. Since he is too old to work in the fields, most of his time is spent in leisure and in conversation with others. His sons are grown and helping him on the farm, and his daughters, who are married by this time, are bringing in cattle as bride price. Truly, the Sisala would say, this is the best time of a man's life. On one occasion, after having talked with a very old woman, my interpreter, a man of about twenty years turned to me and said, "I wish I could be that woman." Somewhat surprised, I asked why and he replied, "Old people have everything. They have things and can give you gifts. We young people, we are poor. We have nothing." This rather extreme statement, involving a cross-sex identification, clearly points out the dominant value orientation attached to age and the process of growing up in the image of one's elders.

The factor of seniority is thus central to the definition of prestige in Sisala society. The Sisala agree that a "successful man" must be both wealthy and generous; he must own many cattle and have many children; he works hard and sees that his "house people" are well fed; he is generous and hospitable to his friends; and he helps those who are poor and unfortunate. This definition of the successful man is clearly related to age, since it is only by growing older that one can legitimately acquire the wealth and authority necessary to be virtuous.

The values attached to age are also reflected in the differences between the funeral (*yoho*) of an old man and that of a young man. When a young person under the age of forty-five dies, his death and the subsequent funeral proceedings are characterized by a mood of deep sorrow. The age mates of the dead man do not attend the burial and funeral for fear that in a moment of sadness they might wish their own deaths and therefore lose their souls (*dima*). No singing or dancing takes place; instead the funeral consists almost solely of the mournful "wailing" of close relatives and friends.

The funeral of an old man, on the other hand, is viewed as an occasion for celebration. Although there is an initial period of mourning or "wailing," it is not characterized by the same deep feeling of pathos. Rather, the funeral is a testimony to the age and achievements of the old man. Friends and age mates come to pay tribute to him through eulogy and sacrifice. All his daughter's husbands and their village people attend and make customary offerings to the dead man's "house people." If the man was old enough to have grown grandchildren and daughter's children, they are also expected to perform customary ceremonies. In contrast to the funeral of a young man, that of an old man is an attestation to his fertility and to the prestige of his house. The Sisala say that when a young man dies, the house is being destroyed; an old man, on the other hand, has already fathered many children, and therefore his death does not diminish the strength of his house.

The funeral of an old man also provides an occasion for the display of

The married daughters of a dead man throw money at their father's funeral.

family wealth and prestige. An old man's funeral is quite large. Those attending it may number as many as 300 to 1000 people, and the proceedings usually last three days. During this time the family of the deceased is expected to care for those who have come to mourn, and money and livestock are given to those who help the family perform the funeral. These include the xylophone players, praise singers, and those responsible for burying the dead. The wealthier the family is, the more it is expected to give.

When a woman marries, she is expected to make a transition from previously held roles as daughter and sister in her own family to the newly acquired roles as wife and mother among her husband's people. Women accept marriage as a necessary condition of their sex and as the only means of gaining self-esteem in a male-dominated and male-oriented culture since by giving birth to children a woman establishes herself as a mother and therefore a builder of her husband's house.

From the viewpoint of the woman marriage and motherhood involve the gradual and often arduous process of transferring her loyalty and identification to her husband's people. During the early period of marriage the wife is regarded as a "stranger" in her husband's house, and she is expected to demonstrate the initiative in establishing amicable relationships with the husband's mother and the other women of the compound. The proper or respectful behavior of women is not seen primarily in terms of the conjugal relationship, but rather in terms of the smooth functioning and welfare of the *janwuo*. The Sisala often say that "bad women" who quarrel "by heart" among themselves can "spoil" a house by creating dissension among brothers. When Sisala men are asked why extended families split apart, the most frequently given reason is quarreling among women. Promiscuous women are also viewed as a threat to the welfare of the husband's house, especially in those cases where the husband is a practitioner of a *tome*-related specialization, since it is believed that an adulterous wife "spoils" her husband's *tome* and may even endanger his life. Thus, a wife's loyalty to her husband's family is closely related to the propriety or impropriety of her behavior.

The stress involved in a women's adjustment to the early years of marriage often leads to divorce. The Sisala say that many young women are troublesome, causing quarrels in the house or running home to their father's people without the permission of their husbands. A divorced woman is held in low esteem by potential suitors as well as by the girl's own family whose prestige suffers by having to return the bride wealth to her former husband's people. A divorced woman may not remarry, in which case she remains in her father's house as a "daughter" (*tolo*). If she becomes promiscuous, which the Sisala say is usually the case with such "bad women," and if such unions lead to the birth of children, the woman must contend with strong ridicule at having borne a bastard. Rather than growing in prestige in her old age by bearing sons to strengthen her husband's family, she brings into the world bastards who will either leave her in search of their real fathers or will cause trouble and dissession in their mother's father's house.

When a woman reaches the age past childbearing, she is called an "elder woman" (*hanihiang*). As with a man, age brings her status in her husband's house, but unlike a man who ascends to propertied authority, her position is based upon her fertility. As an old woman she has grown sons to help with her garden and junior wives to whom she delegates the every day work duties. Her relationship to her husband also becomes closer and less formal. Sisala men say that when a woman grows older, she becomes more like a man, since she is no longer "greedy" like a young woman and takes a greater interest in the affairs of her husband's family. Thus, an elder man often refers to his senior wife as a "mate" and discusses his personal problems with her. Age, then, confers upon a woman a masculine identity based on her service and loyalty to her husband's family.

The value attached to age takes a precedence over those attached to sexual differences, and this is most clearly demonstrated by the funeral of an old woman. Like that of an old man, the funeral takes place in the husband's village. The deceased daughters' husbands are required to attend and make the customary offering of a goat to her husband's people. Friends and even former lovers attend and pay their respects to the husband's "house people." Except for the absence of "funeral sacrifices" (*kuchura*) and the singing of "man songs" (*bayila*), an old woman's funeral is the same as that for an old man. In the case of a woman who was particularly virtuous—for example, the wife of a chief—the funeral may assume proportions larger than that of a man.

INTERPERSONAL RELATIONS: UNITY AND CONFLICT

It has been noted that the Sisala place a high value on politeness and reciprocity in interpersonal relationships. When asked about the characteristics defining the moral conduct of a "good" (*zong*) man, the Sisala reply that a good man is gentle and polite in his behavior, gives respect (*zile*) to all people, avoids quarrels, avoids bringing troubles upon his house, and knows how to keep peace and settle quarrels.

The value placed upon mutual respect and the avoidance of conflict is learned mainly in the context of sibling relationships. That siblings must show one another mutual respect is directly related to the fact that they are the potential co-inheritors of the family wealth and family authority. The Sisala say that when brothers quarrel as children, it is a bad sign, for it means that the house might eventually split apart as a result of dissension. It is believed that a divided house is particularly vulnerable to misfortune. The walls of the *janwuo* and the ancestral shrines contained therein serve to protect the members of the family from the malevolent forces outside. In traditional times if one brother quarreled with another and decided to build his house apart from the main *janwuo*, he ran the risk of being destroyed by wild animals or by the evil deeds of witches (*hila*) who roamed in the night. Since quarreling among brothers is a violation of ancestral custom, family unity and strength is also threatened by the withdrawal of ancestral protection. In recounting tales of warfare the Sisala often attribute the causes of victory to the strength of the ancestors, that is, to ancestors who in their lifetimes had never quarreled. In some funeral songs where death is likened to defeat in warfare the theme of family unity is seen as capable of defeating even death.

The fact that great emphasis is placed upon sibling unity is an admission of the potentiality of conflict and family fission. As the *janwuo* grows in size and as the junior generation succeeds to a position of authority, the previous unity of real siblings becomes a more tenuous unity of siblings and first cousins (that is, father's brother's children). In addition, the death of the last "father" or member of the senior generation releases the members of the junior generation from the authoritarian restrictions which had served to insure sibling solidarity. Brothers and cousins may then begin to quarrel, each asserting his desire to become an "owner" of economic property. One brother, for example, may construct his own granary and begin spending more time tending his private farm than working with his brothers on the family farm. Others of the brothers will follow suit, and thus the *janwuo* becomes divided into a number of economically independent units.

Members of a visiting village dance together at a funeral.

Although the fissive process depends largely upon the idiosyncratic features defining the particular family situation and the relationships among siblings, the overall process is nonetheless governed by the prescriptions of ancestral custom. This is well demonstrated in that aspect of the fissive process involving the ownership of cattle and sheep. Large livestock such as cattle and sheep are called *pungbinu* or "black animals" by the Sisala, and by custom it is only the *diatina* of the *janwuo* who is allowed to own them. If a junior in the house tries to buy these animals secretly and his act is discovered, it is believed that he will die. Thus, a younger brother who desires to own cattle or sheep begins by buying smaller animals such as fowls and goats in order to show others that he is acquiring his own wealth. He also begins picking false quarrels with his elder brothers and cousins, saying that they should not try to exercise control over him. Finally he buys a cow, keeps it secretly in another village, and announces to the elders of his minor lineage that he is going to sacrifice his first cow to the ancestors. After the sacrifice has been performed and the meat shared among everyone in the village, the man's economic independence from his elder brother or cousin, the *diatina,* is affirmed, and henceforth he is allowed to own "black animals."

Although various brothers and cousins of the *diatina* might declare themselves economically independent and form their own *janwuo,* the ritual functions of the larger family or lineage still remain. The shrines and the "ancestral shrine house" (*lele dia*) remain the property of the eldest *diatina,* and all of the brothers attend the sacrifices at these shrines and participate in the division of the sacrificial meat. With the succession of another generation the economic differentiation of the component extended families becomes even more sharply defined, and ritual differentiation, based upon father-to-biological-son inheritance of the custodianship of certain spiritual shrines and medicines, begins to occur. At this point the problem of fission and structural history becomes very complex and goes beyond the scope of this book. Suffice it to say, however, that the fissive process leading to the formation of lesser economic corporate groups is contained within the larger structure, both physical and social, of the minor lineage. In other words, the conflicts leading to the fission of domestic groups are institutionalized within the larger social structure of the society.

This emphasis upon the theme of unity is also reflected in the sphere of intergroup relations within the village. In the average Sisala village, composed of sections of one or more different clans, clan loyalty often exists in opposition to overall loyalty to the village (*jang*). This uneasy alliance of clan sections is counterbalanced by values affirming village unity. The Sisala are very sensitive to divisions within the village and are usually unwilling to discuss these with outsiders, persistently asserting, "We are one." When attending a public function, they always sit together as a village. The origin legends of the various clan sections also serve to promote unity by creating fictive kinship ties among the various clan sections. Clan sections of short time depth, for example, claim kin ties which stem back to the times of the founding of the village. These clan legends and village legends do not mention incidents of intravillage conflict. When the Sisala are asked about obvious divisions existing within the village, they often say that the selfishness and greediness of wives cause brothers to quarrel and families to divide.

In the last analysis, the value of unity and the necessity of avoiding conflicts within both the extended family (*janwuo*) and the village (*jang*) may be explained in the context of Sisala culture history. The Zabirama wars and slave raiding of the latter part of the nineteenth century led to upheavals and major population movements. As a result, the average Sisala village came to be composed of sections of different clans which had historically banded together to provide for their own common defense. The fortified wall around the minor lineage settlement and the highly compact nature of the village attest to this history of warfare. Since the legends of most of the clan sections indicate a foreign origin for their people and even though the migrating clan sections brought with them a section of their clan shrine, it is the shrine of the founding clan of the village or area of land (*tintein*) which serves as protection for all the inhabitants of the village. The migrant clan sections, in addition to their own clan loyalties, were required to form an alliance to the shrine of another clan in order to secure protection in a strange land. This alliance also demanded unity in the face of a common enemy, and the far-reaching clan loyalties had to be sublimated to the immediate concern of village defense. The *jangtina* or "village owner," who is also the *tinteintina* or "land owner," served to mediate conflicts within the village through the auspices of his ritual office as the owner of the "village shrine." For when the Sisala say that "quarrels cause death," they are referring not only to the rational danger of disunity in time of war but also to the mystical danger caused by the withdrawal of protection of the village shrine or spirit in times of intravillage conflict. In short, the strong emphasis placed upon village unity reflects the potential for conflict involved in the often uneasy alliance of disparate clan sections.

It is important to note that the Sisala norms of politeness and decorum in interpersonal relations serve not only to suppress potentially divisive tendencies and shame-producing incidents but also to disguise hostile and evil intentions. As might be suspected in a society which conceals hostility and aggressive impulses, the Sisala have strong beliefs in witchcraft and black magic or "poisoning" (*bera*). Witchcraft is considered a natural phenomenon determined by fate, and it is believed that only a witch is capable of using poisons and other forms of black magic. Whereas female witches (*nyisi*) are always evil, male witches (*hila*) may not be, since a good witch helps to protect his house by being able to detect other witches. Evil witchcraft takes the form of "eating" the "flesh" (*namia*) of a person's soul (*dima*), while black magic consists of the use of "poisons" which may be either placed in the victim's food and drink or projected or "worked" upon the victim at a distance.

Belief in witchcraft and magic also involves the notion of retribution, since witches who participate in groups or covens and share the meat of their victim's soul contract a "meat debt" (*nachima*), meaning that a witch must invite his fellow witches at some later time to participate in the consuming of the soul of a member of his own *janwuo*. To be an evil witch, then, is to destroy the members of one's own family. The same is true of black magic, only in this case retribution is of a mystical nature, for anyone who "poisons" or "works" another will suffer tragedy in his own house, beginning with the illness and death of the younger members.

Beliefs in witchcraft and poisoning represent a projection of interpersonal conflict raised to the level of the supernatural. Whereas brothers who quarrel cause family disunity and breakdown, the practices of witchcraft and poisoning eventually cause its destruction. A witch is evil, the Sisala say, because he cares nothing about his family; conversely, a man who lives alone or whose family has died off is by definition evil, since it is believed that he is responsible for the destruction of its members. The beliefs in witchcraft, therefore, serve to reinforce the interpersonal values of "good" (*zong*) and "evil" (*bong*) by attaching to them a mystical significance.

THE SUPERNATURAL: THE ANCESTORS AND THE SOCIAL ORDER

We can add one further trait to the Sisala definition of the "good man": He gives fear and respect to God and the ancestors. In many respects this relationship to the ancestors is similar to a young man's relationship to his father. To attach causal primacy either to the system of ancestor worship or to the moral prescription of the father-son relationship is of course problematic, but the two relational systems do serve to reinforce one another by providing a continuity between the world of the living and the world of the dead.

This continuity is demonstrated during burial and funeral rites at which time it is believed that the "living soul" (*dima*) of the deceased becomes transformed into a "soul of the dead" (*lelkuome*). An eldest son goes into the grave at the time of burial to see that his father's body is properly placed. Standing on the top of the grave, he says, "Father, we are here to see you go. We will not see you again. So as you go, give us peace in the house. Do not let us suffer from anything at all. Do not let us be disgraced by any other family. Do not bring sickness to our house."

About a week after the funeral, sacrifices are performed by the senior son for the first time in the "ancestor shrine house" of the dead man's *janwuo*. Many of the themes are the same as those at the graveside eulogy except that now the son addresses his father as an ancestor and as a liaison between the worlds of the living and the supernatural. The following sequence of sacrifices is typical.

> Assisted by one of the elder people in his family, the senior son takes a calabash of water and pours a bit on the ground, saying, "Father, you have just left us today. We are now all gathered in front of you, calling you to come and get this water to take to your father, and he to his father. He will assemble all the ancestors. Give them this water to quench their thirst." The senior son then slaughters the first chicken, saying, "This is your food." He then pours water and slaughters a second fowl, saying, "God and his wife the earth and all the gods, we are gathered here in front of our father who has just left us. So we have called him to give him water to quench his thirst. We don't see you, but he has gone to you, and he sees you now. So this is your water too. He will bring it to you. And now we ask you and your wife to give us peace in the house. Give us food and good yield. When we go to the farms, have our children come back laughing. Do not bring sickness to our house. Also let every young man in the house who is not married soon get a wife. Let us have many children in the house. Do not let our house break down (that is, be without children)." Finally, the senior son slaughters a third fowl, calling on the other spirits in the house.

With the final incorporation of the deceased into the world of the ancestors he is no longer prayed or sacrificed to as an individual, and no special shrine is built to commemorate his person. Rather, he is worshipped as part

A cow is sacrificed to the spirit of the departed.

of the larger collectivity of the ancestors. Lacking an elaborate eschatology, the Sisala believe that the ancestors inhabit a village (*lelejang*) which is similar in nature to the human village (*jang*). Some believe that this village is underground; others see it as an invisible village within the human village where the "souls of the dead" walk unnoticed among the living members. The idea of moral judgment in the afterlife is foreign to the Sisala belief system. Instead, it is believed that when the soul of the deceased joins his ancestors, his relationship to them is similar to what it had been when the ancestors were members of the living community. Thus, if the deceased had been a quarrelsome man, he would be reprimanded and disciplined by his seniors in *lelejang,* for the nature of social relationships and the maintenance of social order in the village of the ancestors parallels that of the human community.

The Sisala regard the sacrifice as an act of respect in the sense both of kindness (that is, providing water for the thirsty spirit) and fear. In return they ask or "beg" the ancestors and other deities for protection against misfortune and for the blessings of fertility, wealth, and internal peace. However, the performance of a sacrifice is merely an overt act of respect and is not a sufficient condition for the insurance of good fortune, since the deeper meaning of respect pertains to the adherence to ancestral custom. When a Sisala man says, "I cannot do what my father has not done," he is reaffirming ancestral custom by saying that his adherence to his father's teachings is part of a larger continuous process in which his father also followed the ways of his father. In other words, respect for ancestral custom closely parallels respect for one's father and his teachings, and ancestral custom includes not only the observance of taboos and the proper performance of rituals but also the more general moral problems of respect and amity in human relationships.

Ancestral protection exists in direct relationship to the ritual and moral conduct of the human community, and any breach of custom or act of disrespect threatens its withdrawal. All cases of misfortune and death are eventually attributable to this source, and when they occur, the party involved consults a diviner in order to determine not only how these misfortunes came about but also why they occurred. The interpretation of misfortune in terms of the violation of ancestral custom is clearly pointed up in the following case:

> In a minor lineage settlement in the village of Sorbelle two elder men died in close succession. Prior to the latter's burial a diviner was consulted to determine the cause of death. He stated that the two old men had had a quarrel over the marriage of one of the "daughters" in the house and that in a moment of heated argument both swore (*kabre*) on the ancestors. Since it is a violation of ancestral custom to quarrel about the betrothal and marriage of daughters and since swearing on the ancestors is an awesome and dangerous thing to do, both of the old men died. The diviner then added that the quarrel did not die with the old men, and that more people would die unless measures were taken to rectify the internal dissension within the house.

In sum, the ancestors and the various shrines which they have entrusted to the community of the living provide the element of order in an indeterminate and dangerous world. This order, as defined by ritual customs and the moral axioms of human relationships, is maintained by the threat of the withdrawal of ancestral protection. Perception of misfortune in terms of ancestral wrath serves as a powerful agent of social control, and conversely, the blessings of fertility, wealth, and peace are interpreted as stemming from a people's proper relationship with their ancestors.

Means of social control within the human community are directly related to beliefs in the power of the ancestors to maintain the social order. The process of human justice is concerned with repairing relationships more than with absolute pronouncements of right and wrong. It functions to prevent disputes and violations of custom from reaching serious proportions which would incur the displeasure of the ancestors. Within the village setting neither violence nor the threat of violence was traditionally used to maintain order, for the ultimate sanction resided in the awesome and absolute power of the ancestors and other spiritual deities.

Minor disputes are settled by the elder persons having jurisdiction over the litigants. Disputes involving members of the same clan section are heard by the eldest man of the clan section, while those of members of different clan sections are heard by the *jangtina* and his elders. These disputes most commonly involve either property or marriage, and reference is always made to tradition. The judicial authority of the elder man or *jangtina* stems from the wisdom of his age and his ability to interpret the true ways of the ancestors. To refuse to abide by his decision would be a gross act of disrespect and a violation of ancestral custom which would place the individual in mortal danger.

If disputes cannot be settled through informal consensus or if they reach truly serious proportions, the Sisala believe that the spiritual shrines in the village will be "spoiled." When the Sisala say that quarrels cause death, they are referring to the mystical connection between the moral misconduct of human beings and the withdrawal of ancestral and spiritual protection. If a diviner discovers that a shrine in the village is "angry," an effort is made to determine the cause. If a serious conflict or the practice of witchcraft is involved, the "owner of the shrine" (*venetina*) asks the guilty or suspected parties to bring livestock to placate the shrine. When the animals are sacrificed, the person whose guilt or complicity is known is expected to "swear" an oath upon the shrine, stating that he will reform or at least desist from doing those things which caused the shrine to become angry. In cases where it is not possible to determine the guilty party, such as in cases of witchcraft, the person suspected to doing evil is expected to swear to the veracity of his statement. In either case if the individual swears falsely, it is believed that his death is imminent. After the sacrifice the sacrificial meat is divided and shared among all the family heads of either the clan section (in the case of the clan section shrine) or the village (in the case of the village shrine).

Individual moral misconduct is thus the concern of all members of the community, since such behavior may cause the withdrawal of supernatural protection. Oath swearing serves to release the community from this state of danger by placing the burden of guilt and its consequences upon the individual. However, the guilty person is nonetheless a kinsman, and his actions reflect upon the status of his family, lineage, and village. The larger function of oath taking and sacrifice, then, is the reparation of relationships within the human community so that further incidents may be avoided. The sharing of the sacrificial meat among the various families of the village is an act of generosity and mutual respect aimed at mending both the present and perhaps previous unresolved conflicts. Even in cases of witchcraft, assuming that supernatural justice does not take its toll, the individual is given a second chance and is reintegrated into the everyday affairs of his people.

4/The modern educational experience: the older generations

EUROPEAN CONTACT AND THE SISALA REACTION

The Sisala's perception of the white man and their reaction to his presence must be understood in terms of their recent history. As previously noted, the Sisala have had a tradition of military defeat by the militarily more powerful Zabirama people whose rule caused the upheaval and displacement of great segments of the population. These defeats left the people war weary and devastated by the famine and severe epidemics caused by living in crowded fortifications. During the 1890s, when Zabirama rule had become particularly oppressive, the British made their first appearance in the Sisala area and with the aid of the Sisala defeated the Zabirama in 1897. This opportune defeat of the Zabirama was therefore regarded as an act of liberation, and the Sisala offered no resistance to subsequent British occupation of their territory. Even today old men sing the praises of the white man for defeating the Zabirama and for allowing the people to return to their land.

By his defeat of the Zabirama the white man came to be perceived as having provided the benefits of "civilization." This notion, however, refers not only to the obvious material and technological innovations accepted by the Sisala but also to an important concept concerning the acquisition of knowledge and the contracting of social relationships. It is often said that a man must travel beyond his village to acquire "sense," for it is only by traveling that a person can form new relationships and thereby learn about the world about him. This is also related to the rationale given for village exogamy, since the marriage of each daughter of a given family involves the contracting of a new set of affinal relationships. During the time of the Zabirama wars men could not travel safely beyond their villages, and the rule of village endogamy or inmarriage prevailed out of necessity. The performance of the funeral, so central to family prestige, must also have been limited because of restrictions on travel and on widely based affinal relationships. The coming of the white man thus meant not only freedom from oppression but also freedom to carry out the "civilized" functions of society as the Sisala perceived them.

It would be wrong to assume that the Sisala were unaware of the past abuses of colonialism; however, it is important to note that these abuses were minimal, since the British presence, as far as the people perceived it, did not usually interfere with their everyday affairs. For the most part, the colonial officer had very little face-to-face contact with the Sisala, relegating the everyday enforcement of his directives to African constables. If the people felt they were being treated unjustly, they tended to blame the African representatives of the colonial administration rather than the British themselves. Also since the British were concerned mainly with the "pacification" of the area and not with the economic exploitation of its people and resources, many of the injustices associated with colonialism, such as the involuntary expropriation of land and conscription of labor, were at a minimum. Thus, the white man in his position of isolation was perceived as uninvolved in the everyday affairs and conflicts of the people, and the reality of European social institutions and values remained essentially vague and meaningless.

Notwithstanding British ignorance of Sisala custom and the ineffectiveness of their administration, they did establish one significant and far-reaching change in the traditional order: the institution of chieftaincy under the colonial policy of Indirect Rule. Throughout Africa the British sought to administer their rule through the establishment of native authorities. These authorities were supposed to represent the traditional political structure of

The chief of Tumu arrives at a funeral in Tumu.

headmen, chiefs, and paramount chiefs. Ideally this system worked best in those societies which had centralized and hierarchical political systems. In these cases the British colonial officer would administer his directives to a head or paramount chief who in turn would affect their enforcement upon the lesser chiefs and village headmen. However, in societies without indigenous hierarchies the institution of chieftaincy was an arbitrary imposition which often led to deep conflicts and changes in the traditional order.

In the case of the Sisala this hierarchical system of secular chieftaincy was without precedent, since traditional legitimate authority was mainly ritual in nature and never extended beyond the village except during times of warfare. In the imposed system each village had a chief and these chiefs in turn were subordinate to "subdivisional chiefs" of which there were twelve in the Tumu District. At the top of the hierarchy was the chief of Tumu (Tumukuoro) who was appointed by the British as paramount chief of the Sisala people.

The rise of chieftaincy and the social dynamics involved in the process varied from village to village. Sisala elder men often recall that at sometime in the past the British had come to their villages and requested a representative. In most cases the *jangtina* (village owner) was offered by the village people. If he was a very old person, which was often the case, the district commissioner demanded a younger person who would be a more capable administrator. In this event a younger member of the family or minor lineage of the *jangtina* would be selected. In villages where more than one dominant clan section existed or where one lineage or clan section had achieved a position of power as a result of the Zabirama wars, the issue of chieftaincy frequently led to conflict resulting in permanent divisions between the lineage of the *jangtina* and that of the chief (*kuoro*). The British insistence upon father-son succession also posed problems since it ran contrary to the Sisala pattern of succession based on relative age. Succession to the office of chieftaincy was, and still is, a matter involving conflict.

The exact origin of the office of subdivisional chief is not known since the British left no account of their method of selection. The only criterion applicable to all twelve subdivisional chieftaincies is that they were located in villages of relatively high total population. Although many conflicts arose concerning the legitimacy of the subdivisional chiefs, the location of the office, with one exception, has not changed throughout the course of modern Sisala history, and this probably stems from the support the British gave the subdivisional chiefs and the powers they entrusted in them. The subdivisional chiefs in turn supported both the British and the chief of Tumu who were responsible for the legitimazation of their power. Given the authority to organize public works and levy fines as well as the extralegal prerogatives of accepting bribes, the wealth and power of the subdivisional chiefs was substantial.

It would be wrong to assume that the power gained by chiefs stemmed solely from the indirect exercise of British authority, for also involved is the mystical concept of fate and the relationship between the attainment of wealth and a man's possession of supernatural power. It has been shown that the wealth and prosperity of a family is believed to be directly related to the beneficence and power of the family's ancestral and spiritual shrines, and that an individual's personal wealth and power are related to the strength of his personal spirits (*tome*) and medicines (*dalusun*). Since many chiefs became wealthy through their administration of British authority, the people attributed their good fortune to fate and to personal magical powers, and thus the power of the chiefs became less and less dependent upon the British.

This is most clearly demonstrated in the rise to power of Kanton, chief of Tumu and paramount chief of the Sisala, who ruled from 1918 until his death in 1951. The immediate former chief of Tumu was a very old man and, by British standards, an incapable administrator. When he died, it was arranged that he be succeeded by one of his sons, Kanton. Although the British were impressed by Kanton's ability and loyalty, the other subdivisional chiefs were not, and many refused to swear allegiance to him. Within a period of three years, however, Kanton rose to a position of almost absolute power which he maintained until his death. Subsequent district commissioners noted that whenever Kanton issued an order, it was promptly executed by his subordinate chiefs, and although some distrusted his political motives, none complained about his abilities. To explain Kanton's power purely in terms of his association with the British would be inaccurate since during the period of his ascendancy the British no longer lived in Tumu.

Fortunately an historical document of significant value recorded by a colonial officer has been preserved. It describes one of perhaps many such events which help to explain Kanton's rise to power.

> In 1921, Mahama, the chief of Bellu [a village of a subdivisional chieftaincy] had collected a certain following of chiefs, and among the masses it was known that this Mahama had come to the meeting of chiefs armed with powers superior to Kanton the chief of Tumu. Thousands of people had assembled to witness the confrontation. Suddenly, there was a great panic, and the people ran away in fright. The cause of the panic was due to the fact that Mahama of Bellu's hat fell to the ground; which apparently demonstrated to the crowd that Kanton's power was superior to that of Mahama, and that the magic contained in Mahama's hat was a menace to them. Some days later, on the return of the Acting Provincial Commissioner from Wa, the meeting was held and every chief was loud in his praises of Kanton, whom they regarded as their paramount chief ever since, and I would add that his "magic" power still awed all and sundry up to the time I left the district in 1929 (Eyre-Smith 1933:39).

The fact that Kanton's power was believed to be derived from his personal supernatural powers is unanimously held by the Sisala. When Kanton was alive, it was said that elder men trembled in fear in his presence and that his curse meant immediate death. When he died, many people did not come immediately to his funeral because they could not believe that he had actually died. Kanton's power also extended to his family and village. The village shrine of Tumu, the Tumuwihiye, was regarded as the most powerful shrine in the Sisala area.

The main effect of British contact from 1906 to 1946 was to create a political system based upon the dual authority of the chief and *jangtina*. The authority of the *jangtina* is ritual in nature based upon his custodianship of the village shrine and his descent from the founding lineage; and his duty is to act in conjunction with the village elders in order to affect village harmony. The power of the chief, on the other hand, stems from the acquisition of personal wealth and charismatic power. The secular and ritual maintenance of intravillage unity has been largely transformed into a system of authority based upon the maintenance of alliances and relationships of ingratiation. Although the *jangtina* has retained his ritual prerogatives, many of his previously held secular rights and privileges, such as the adjudication of intravillage disputes, have been taken over by the chiefs. However, as indicated below, the legitimazation of the powers of the chief has never been fully integrated with the traditional concepts of authority based on age.

MIGRATION: THE MIGRANT'S EXPERIENCE AND HIS ADJUSTMENT

As mentioned previously, the Sisala people were particularly isolated during the early years of colonial rule. During the 1910s and 1920s relatively few Sisala moved out of their local areas, and those who did were often conscripted into the police or army. Although no statistics exist for the period, migration outside the tribal area probably did not begin until the late 1930s as motorized transport centers arose in the neighboring towns of Bolgatanga and Wa.

The postwar period witnessed a substantial increase in Sisala migration, especially to the major urban centers of the South such as Kumasi and Accra. According to the 1960 census (Ghana Census Office 1964) there were 59,210 Sisala, and of these, 9,270 lived outside of the "tribal area" (that is, Tumu, Wa, and Lawra Districts of the Upper Region). Of the latter group about one-third had been born outside the native area, while about two-thirds migrated from the North. In the years which have passed since the census this number has undoubtedly increased. It is difficult to estimate from the statistics what percentage of the Sisala migrants remain in the South and establish residence, and what percentage eventually return to the tribal area. In my own informal census I found that about 70 percent of the people between the ages of twenty and fifty living in Tumu and the surrounding villages had at sometime traveled outside the Sisala area. Of these about 50 percent had remained for a substantial period of time before returning home.

Because of their lack of education and technical training, most migrants engage in common labor. About one-half live in urban areas over 5000 people, and the urban sex ratio is about three males for every two females, reflecting the transitory nature of urban migration. The rural migrant, on the other hand, tends to be more sedentary, establishing a household with his wife and children and engaging in cash crop farming or the commercial production of charcoal.

Migration is a very important factor in the presence of sociocultural change among the Sisala, since it provides the primary human link joining the Sisala to the modern world, as defined by the acculturated and urban South. The locus of this change process lies in the returning migrant's adaptation to village life and in his relationships with others in the traditional social environment.

When a man returns from having lived in the South, he is initially regarded with admiration. If he has been fortunate, he returns dressed in finery and bearing gifts for his family and kin. His friends invite him to their houses or treat him to beer or *pito* on market days, and in this setting he tells stories about his adventures and the things he saw in the South. Such a man is regarded with admiration, and most migrants maintain that their decision to travel was based upon stories they had heard from former migrants.

Beneath these surface explanations, however, lies a deeper motivation involving the desire to ownership and economic independence. One young migrant living in Accra explained his feelings as follows:

> When I was living in my father's house, there was nothing to do but help my father on the farm. If I worked my own farm and sold what I had grown in the market, I had to show respect to my father by giving him the money I earned. And if I wanted to buy a cloth or buy beer for my friends on market day, I would have to beg my father for money. I may be poor now, but at least I own my own clothes. And if I want to buy beer for my friends, I don't have to ask my father.

Migration to the South thus provides a means of bypassing the traditional age-status system by allowing the young man sufficient economic autonomy to acquire the material symbols of wealth and prestige. To this may be added the young man's perception of the returning migrant as against his perception of himself as a poor farmer. Each factor reinforces the other; one provides the underlying motivation and the other a direction for the expression of this motivation.

The impetus for migration is also related to factors leading to familial fission. As long as a man's father or his father's brothers are living, he is not free to make any serious decision such as migration without their permission. However, when the last member of his father's generation dies and the patrimony passes to the senior member of his own generation, sibling tensions heretofore held in abeyance come into the open. In the traditional setting such tensions led to familial fission; in the contemporary setting they often result in migration.

When a man migrates to the South, he seeks the aid of kinsmen. In the multitribal urban setting, however, fellow villagers and even tribesmen are referred to as "brothers," and the fraternal values of unity and mutual assistance are strived for in intratribal relationships. Each of the migrant communities has a Sisala "zongo chief," and he helps to facilitate the new migrant's adjustment by providing temporary housing, financial assistance, and often a job. In Mamobi there is also a Sisala mutual aid society, Sisala Padongngo or "Sisala help-each-other," which provides assistance and guidance for its members.

Notwithstanding the aid given by tribesmen, great demands are placed upon the migrant's initiative in contracting relationships and securing a livelihood. As one migrant put it: "When I was living with my father, my food was free, my room was free. Here everything costs money." Employment is always a problem, and loans from small-scale creditors frequently lead to a cycle of perpetual debt. In order to gain his basic subsistance a Sisala man must often resort to women's work such as carrying water and firewood or pounding yams. Hopes of buying nice clothing and gifts must be often abandoned, and the need for money may result in anxiety and humiliation. As a result many migrants remain in the South to spare themselves the further humiliation of returning home in poverty.

The Sisala frequently say that in the South they are strangers on another's land and that they must abide by his rules. In the case of Mamobi the land and many of the compounds rented by the Sisala are owned by the Ga chief of the area. Being a "stranger," however, has deeper implications. In the North the Sisala man is the "owner" (*tina*) of not only his land and his house but also his shrines and gods. When he migrates, the entire complex of customs and institutions revolving around the concept of "ownership" becomes incompatible with his new role. These would include the system of land tenure based upon economically corporate compounds, the complex of religious beliefs connected with the land or with specific locations and natural phenomena, and the whole system of political authority—both ritual and secular—which is based upon the ownership and control of the land. To be a "stranger" (*nihouro*) means not only to be disenfranchised but also to be placed in a state of imminent danger without the protection of one's ancestors and protective medicines.

One of the responses to this situation has been an increase in conversion to Islam and to a lesser degree, Christianity. According to the 1960 census (Ghana Census Office 1964), 49.4 percent of the Sisala living in "urban" areas of more than 5000 people are Moslems as opposed to 8.4 percent in "rural areas." A similar differentiation also exists for Christianity with 11.55 percent in urban areas and 5.2 percent in rural areas. When the Sisala in Accra are asked why they converted to Islam, they say that in the South a man is not protected by his "fetishes" at home, that the South is a dangerous place, and that one needs the protection of Islam. For many, especially the short-term migrant, "conversion" to Islam consists primarily of procuring protective charms from Moslem holy men, and when they return to the North, they disregard their Islamic practices. However, while in the South, Islam serves to provide the protection and security in an unpredictable and dangerous world.

Affiliation with Islam also has the larger function of providing an identity nexus for the members of diverse northern tribes living in the South. When the northerner comes to the South, he encounters ethnic prejudice. In addition to being made aware of his low educational and occupational status, he is called "bush" or "primitive" by his more acculturated southern countrymen. The social pressures to conform to Islam represent a reaction to this prejudice, and Islam provides both a source of social cohesion for members of diverse northern tribes and a means of escaping an undesirable ethnic self-image.

The Moslems of Tumu perform public prayers.

The migrant's experience in the South and his identification with Islam and the larger community of northern tribes create the basis of a cosmopolitan-like identity. When the migrant returns home, he sees himself as a man who has traveled, who has gained firsthand knowledge of the hardships of life and who has acquired the knowledge or "sense" necessary to cope with today's problems and "today's people" (*jining nia*). The man who does not travel, on the other hand, does not acquire real "sense," since he has never had to face the world unaided by his kinsmen. Life in the South is seen as building character, a character borne of suffering and of an awareness of how things are, an awareness of reality. The returning migrant also sees himself as more "civilized." Habits of personal cleanliness, the use of eating utensils, and the desire for nice clothing all represent changes in his life style which set him apart from his unacculturated tribesmen.

The following statement by a young Sisala migrant is a typical Sisala evaluation of experiences in the South.

> In Tumu, there are people who have never been anywhere. They don't know anything. They haven't seen anything. They just listen to what people say. They are blind. This place is not like the South. Because when you go down South, you see a lot of forest, traffic is very much, you see a lot of story buildings. There you can learn something like a trade. Here you can't learn anything. In that place you mix with different people; and if you are good, you can learn different languages. When you are down South, you can eat, sleep, and bathe whenever you want and nobody cares. But when you stay near your parents, you won't learn anything. Here you just ask your mother or your brother's wives for food and they give it to you. Down South you have to work for these things. And so it is good for one to go to different towns. When I was very young and had not been to the South, I didn't really know anything at all. But when I went and saw so many things—if I had not been there, I would never have known these things. I would never have learned a trade. In the South I took a bath twice a day and used to get dressed up. In the evening I would go and watch games, football and horse races. I used to go to the cinema to see different kinds of activities. On my return to Tumu, I was able to get a sewing machine. I also got some dresses and some furniture. You could never get things like this through farming. There are many men like me down South because of such things. When one

Import and industrial items on sale in Tumu's market.

stays here, you can't have anything, know anything, or get a good job. That is what makes our people travel to other places.

While the migrant seeks to impress his unacculturated tribesmen and to perpetuate a positive image of his life in the South, his self-conception is tempered by an awareness of his position in the larger society. While living in the South, he becomes increasingly aware of the differences in wealth between the rich and the poor. The image of the "big man," living in a two-story house and driving a black Mercedes-Benz, is beyond the expectation of the migrant. The life of the "big man," like that of the white man, is viewed as one of leisure and except for its outer manifestations, is incomprehensible to the average Sisala. Thus, the migrant sees himself as a "poor man," both as a farmer in the North and as a zongo dweller in the South, and so he resigns himself to the life of the farmer, laborer, artisan, or trader.

The migrant's belief in "fate" and his attitude toward work help to explain the returning migrant's adjustments to the traditional routine of village life. His initial prestige on return lessens as the money he earned in the South runs out. If he has acquired a trade, he tries to practice it as best he can, and thus it is not unusual to find sewing machines and accomplished tailors in Sisala villages. The practice of such trades, however, is at best only part-time specialization, and the migrant must eventually return to farming. Although some attempt is made to retain aspects of Islam (such as the performance of prayers), by far the greatest percentage of returned migrants forsake their Islamic beliefs for the renewed protection of their ancestral spirits and shrines. Since many migrants marry soon after their return from the South, traditional domestic obligations also reassert their hold. To a large extent, then, migration is a temporary discontinuity in the life of a Sisala man, and the knowledge acquired in the South becomes meaningless in light of his rapid readaptation to village life.

In recent times, however, changes have taken place in the returning migrant's pattern of adjustment, largely because of post-World War II developments in the town of Tumu. Prior to this time Tumu, except for the fact that it was the seat of the paramount chieftaincy, was similar to other Sisala villages with respect to its degree of modernization. When the government station was closed in 1920, Tumu reverted to a virtually completely traditional village. Aside from the minor lineage settlements of the crow clan (*gilinganviara*) indigenous to the town, no other settlements, buildings, or other manifestations of the European presence existed. The traders and foreigners who resided in Tumu prior to 1920 left with the British, and Tumu declined as a center of trade and diffusion of European culture.

In 1946 the government station was reopened, and with this event came the reestablishment of government services, the constablary, and renewed trade in the district. Moslem Hausa and Yoruba traders and artisans, living in the larger commercial centers such as Wa, began moving into Tumu. Purchasing land from the chief of Tumu, they helped to establish the Tumu zongo or "strangers' settlement." Gradually Tumu became the major trading center in the district. During the 1950s these changes accelerated steadily: a Baptist mission was established in 1952 to be followed soon after by a Catholic mission; followers of orthodox and later Ahmadiyya Islam, many of whom were Hausa and Yoruba, built mosques; and the Tumu primary boarding school, which was built in 1945, was followed by the establishment of other schools, including two middle schools and a teacher training college. After independence in 1957 the government established public works corporations, State Farms and the Workers Brigade, which along with the clerical and teaching positions already in existence offered opportunities for wage employment. By 1960 what had been a traditional village was now a modern town with a zongo or "stranger" population of well over 1000 persons.

The greater part of this "stranger" population is made up of Sisala who originally came from other villages, consisting of teachers, government employees, retired government employees on pension (mostly former constables and soldiers), and former migrants who had lived for some time in the South and who subsequently chose to reside in Tumu either for reasons of economic independence or because of their Islamic affiliation. In addition, a large percentage of this population consists of native Tumu people who have broken away from their larger minor lineage settlements and have established independent households in the zongo section of Tumu. These individuals and their families usually live in modern rectangular compounds which they share with other, often unrelated, family units. They gain their livelihood by farming land granted to them by the chief of Tumu, taking wage employment in the Workers' Brigade and State Farms, practicing a trade such as tailoring or masonry, or becoming small scale traders and entrepreneurs.

In contrast to the villages, the Sisala of Tumu state that they can come close to maintaining themselves in a style of life similar to that which they were accustomed in the South. This advantage is manifest in the possession of such material items as bicycles, European clothing, dishes and eating utensils, articles of furniture such as chairs and a bed, and items of personal hygiene such as soap and pomades. In addition, by gaining employment or engaging in entrepreneurial activity the individual is able to maintain himself economically without becoming involved in the subsistence activities of his larger extended family. Thus, it is reasonable to assume that the motivations responsible for the Sisala settlement of Tumu zongo are similar to those underlying southward migration.

It would be wrong, however, to assume that a Sisala man living in Tumu zongo is able to maintain complete economic independence from his kinsmen, since kin relationships are highly diffuse and not easily separated from their economic aspects. From time to time a man requires help of his kin, especially for the performance of customary rites and obligations. In order for a Sisala man to marry he must gain the support and consent of his patrilineal kin, and even if he could independently raise sufficient funds for the bride wealth, he is restricted by custom from purchasing a cow since the ownership of cattle is the sole prerogative of his family headman (*dia-tina*). He also requires the services of his family for the naming of his children and for help with funerary obligations, and in return for these services he is expected to help his family. As a wageworker he may be obliged to furnish money for payment of the annual "head tax" or for bribing police and court officials in a legal case involving his family. If he is moderately wealthy, he may be entrusted with the education and discipline of one of his brother's children. Thus, the economic independence of the Sisala living in Tumu zongo is more apparent than real; unless one wishes to sever all ties with his kin, reciprocity invariably remains.

Perhaps more important than the partial attainment of economic independence is the former migrant's view of himself in relation to the rest of society. The fact that he is able to maintain a relatively elaborate life style serves as a sign of his position as a traveled and "civilized" man; likewise, the retention of Islamic practices and the formation of relationships with fellow Moslems also constitutes a symbol of his new identity.

This fact is demonstrated by recent changes in the villages outside Tumu where the former migrant is closely tied to the subsistence activities and economic pursuits of his extended family. Despite these ties attempts are made to maintain the modern life style. Former migrants frequently give their children Islamic or Christian names in addition to the Sisala names, and in many of the villages, especially those situated along roads, acculturated Sisala have built small houses of two or three rooms inhabited by nuclear or polygynous family units. This tendency toward the establishment of small household units is well expressed in the following statement.

> Since I am a Moslem, I can stay anyplace. So I asked permission from my elders to build a house here. My brothers helped me build it. Besides, the compound was getting too crowded for me. The Moslem religion does not allow for sacrifices and things like that. There are certain things they do in the house [i.e., his extended family] that my religion does not allow. I am very fond of Moslems. And so living near the road like this, I can attract more Moslem friends who, like me, maybe would not like to live in his family's compound. And so if any Moslem passes by, he can stop and say prayers with me. I can also offer any stranger a drink of water and a place to stay for the night. Gradually, I feel that more strangers and Moslems will come to settle in my village and there will be a zongo right in the area where I live.

Reflected in this statement are the underlying motivations of the former migrant: the need to control his own property and affairs and the need to maintain a cosmopolitan identity through the formation of a wide range of extrakin and extratribal relationships.

SCHOOLS, POLITICS, AND THE EARLY LITERATES

In the early years of the colonial administration no serious attempts were made to educate the Sisala people. Although some British colonial officers suggested the possibility of boarding schools, the Sisala reacted unfavorably to the idea of sending their children away to the South. By 1931 only one person in the Tumu District had been educated (Gold Coast Census Office 1932), but during the latter 1930s, primary boarding schools were built in Lawra, Wa, and Bolgatanga, and a middle boarding school was constructed in the regional capital of Tamale. Those Sisala who went to school between 1935 and 1945 attended these boarding schools outside the district. In 1945 the first primary school in the Tumu District was built in the town of Tumu itself, but by 1948 there were still only twenty-eight Sisala with six or more years of education (Gold Coast Census Office 1950:352–353).

Those educated during this time delight in recalling their school experiences. They mention that they had to walk seventy miles in bare feet to attend the school in Lawra where they lived with children of other northern tribes in the school compound and were taught by African teachers from the South. Order and discipline in the classrooms were strictly enforced, and the children were beaten not only for disrespect or violation of rules, but also for inability to give correct answers to their teachers' questions. Vacations occurred once or twice yearly, and again the children made the round trip between Lawra and Tumu on foot. The older educated say that when they went to school, things were more difficult, the discipline was stricter, and students studied harder and with a greater sense of accomplishment.

The parents of the older educated Sisala were illiterate and for the most part, untraveled and unacculturated. They knew little of schools except that they were institutions of the white man. The school boy was called the "white man's child" and his education, including discipline, was entrusted to the white man. Parents felt that education was an investment which would enhance the family's prestige by producing a young adult who stood in an ingratiating relationship to the white man. As the literate member of the community the schoolboy was regarded as a liaison between his elder men and the colonial government serving as messenger and interpreter. Beyond this, education was perceived as meaningless, and the schoolboy was expected to conform to the same work requirements and moral conduct as his illiterate brothers.

Although the schoolboy learned knowledge and skills which prepared him for an occupation alien to his traditional world, he nonetheless initially accepted the role expectations of his parents. The older educated often say that they had greater respect for their parents and other senior people than do members of the younger generation. They attended school because their parents desired them to do so, and it was always their goal to serve their families. As one man put it, "Every family has its people who hunt and its people who farm. In the same way every family has its educated people."

In the primary boarding school established in Tumu in 1945 the teachers were all Sisala, and with few exceptions none was educated beyond the middle school. A gradual interest in education developed, and by 1950 primary schools had been built in three more villages with Sisala headmasters drawn from the original Tumu primary school.

The rapid growth of schools during this period also meant a rapid rise in the prestige of the small group of educated Sisala whose ages ranged between fifteen and thirty at the time of the opening of the Tumu primary school. The Sisala literates developed a strong sense of unity based in part upon common school experiences and in part upon a common feeling of purpose and mission, the latter dedicated to rasing the status of their people by achieving high standards in education. Emphasis in teaching was placed upon competitiveness among students and the achievement of high scores on the primary school leaving examinations. Aware of the high educational standards in other parts of the Gold Coast, the teachers conceived their personal aspirations in terms of their tribal identity.

The chiefs of Tumu and the other villages took an active interest in the schools and were instrumental in supplying labor for their construction. When the Tumu primary school was opened in 1945, a council of elders was created to supervise school policy. The elder men often sat in the back of the classroom, and although they were not able to understand English, they nonetheless observed whether the proper relationship between students and teachers was being maintained. If the elder men made an unfavorable report to the chief of Tumu (the Tumukuoro), the particular students and teachers concerned were forced to answer to him. Frequently the Tumukuoro and his elders made food inspections at the school, and if there was work to do at the school, the Tumukuoro called the whole town together to participate in communal labor.

While the literate minority viewed themselves as the educators and reformers of their people, the chiefs and their elders saw the literates as a liaison between themselves and a modern world which they were just able to perceive. The literates accepted the role expectations of their elders and their elder's manifest control over the school system. Their aspirations for personal power and prestige, whether or not they were consciously realized at this time, were kept in abeyance, and between 1945 and 1950 no apparent conflict of interest emerged between the literates and the traditional authority. However, in 1951 and 1952 two events occurred which caused a profound alteration in this relationship: the death of Kanton and the institution of the Local Government Ordinance, respectively.

Prior to Kanton's death the native authority system in the Tumu District consisted of a "state council" made up of the twelve subdivisional chiefs, headed by the Tumukuoro; its primary concern lay in the maintenance and enforcement of colonial directives. During this time Kanton was indisputably the most powerful man in the Tumu District, and although he was despised by some, all swore allegiance to him. However, when his elder son succeeded him, the subdivisional chiefs stated that they no longer wished to follow Tumu. As a result, the British modified the Tumu Native Authority into a confederacy consisting of twelve subdivisional chiefs under the presidency of the Tumukuoro who occupied the position of first among equals. Never again would the Tumu District and the Sisala people show the same unity they had enjoyed while Kanton was living.

The Local Government Ordinance of 1951 was an important manifestation of the growing nationalistic impetus toward independence in Ghana, for as the Gold Coast approached the time of independence many educated Africans felt that the native authority system, with its alliance between chiefs and district commissioners, could only lead to the further entrenchment of colonialism. The Local Government Ordinance then modified the previous system by the creation of "district councils" which in turn would be made up of smaller "local councils." With two-thirds of their membership elected by the people and one-third appointed by the traditional authorities, both these councils were charged with the responsibility for public education, local water supply, clinics and dispensaries, and the maintenance of local roads. The "state councils" existed simultaneously with the new local government system, but their functions were limited to traditional matters.

That the Local Government Ordinance constituted a threat to the power of the Sisala confederacy of subdivisional chiefs was not at first realized. In April 1952, elections were held to determine the representatives of the Tumu District Council and six local councils; as of June 1952, the Tumu District Council consisted of six traditional members, twelve representative members (two from each of the six local councils), and the Tumukuoro as president. Since the composition of the state council remained unchanged, the chiefs assumed that they retained their former powers and therefore refused to take advantage of their right to select a third of the members of the district council. Instead they appointed two minor chiefs and four literates to serve as their intermediaries. However, the chiefs soon realized that the state council no longer had the authority to collect revenue, and they regretted their oversight but it was too late.

The power of the chiefs was also weakened by the disunity resulting from Kanton's death. While the Tumu District Council functioned efficiently, largely because of its literate membership, the small local councils did not fare so well. Each local council was composed of one to three subdivisional chieftaincies, with the presidency rotating among the component subdivisional chiefs. Since the chiefs favored moves toward decentralization, greater attention was given to the local councils than to the district council, but this concern was generally not very constructive. For the most part, the chiefs quarrelled over the location of the local council office, each wanting it in his own village for the sake of prestige. This move toward decentralization also weakened the alliance of village chiefs toward their subdivisional superiors, thereby compounding an already confusing situation. While the chiefs were occupied with matters of prestige and propriety, the practical matters of government such as sanitation and education were left to the literate members, and they were the ones who represented the local councils at meetings of the district council.

Thus, the literate group of Sisala readily gained control of the district council; moreover, they were more unified and far better equipped to handle the practical problems of government. During meetings the younger literates opposed the chiefs in debate, but in accordance with tradition the chiefs either left the meeting or kept quiet in fear of losing the argument and thereby being disgraced. Democratic procedures based upon debate and majority rule were foreign to traditional political behavior based on respect for status and decision by unanimous consensus; eventually many chiefs refused to attend meetings or have anything to do with the district council.

The chiefs and elder men, however, did retain power, particularly in their ability to determine the voting patterns of their respective constituencies. Any literate aspiring to an elected office was forced to appeal to the traditional authority figures who in turn told their people how to vote. Generally the criteria for election to local or national office had nothing to do with contemporary political issues. Ties of kinship and friendship, along with the ability to speak and the demonstration of respectful behavior, were most important. The literate politician also had to be able to reduce or translate the main issues of nationalism and modernization into terms understandable to his constituency. If the candidate was able to meet these criteria, the elder men of the village sat in council and came to a unanimous decision; the whole village then voted for the single candidate.

The interrelationship between the literates and the traditional authority is well demonstrated in the Sisala's participation in national politics. In 1950 in anticipation of the independence of the Gold Coast a preliminary constitution was written which established a parliamentary body called the Legislative Assembly, and a general election was held in 1951 to determine its representatives. The Tumu District was supposed to elect one representative, but Kanton chose instead to appoint one of his educated sons to the position. No one, including the British district commissioner, disputed his right to override the electoral procedure.

Between 1951 and the election of a new Legislative Assembly in 1954 national politics generated a great deal of interest in the Tumu District. With the decentralization of authority following Kanton's death a multiplicity of political factions arose, some affiliating with national and regional parties, others forming local splinter parties. Party affiliation, however, was dictated by traditional concerns and alliances more than by national issues and ideology. Thus, traditional disputes and antagonisms between clan sections of a given village or between two subdivisional chieftaincies found expression in national politics. The candidates for the new Legislative Assembly, while representing the nationalistic platforms of their parties, also represented the vested interests of those chiefs who were allied behind them. The chiefs expected the literate to use his influence in their behalf in matters of local dispute and to help them gain access to such benefits as school buildings and scholarships for their young.

By 1954 the Tumu District was divided among three major political parties and a number of smaller splinter parties. One of these parties was the Convention Peoples Party (CPP) under the leadership of Kwame Nkrumah, and prior to the 1954 general election Nkrumah came to the Tumu

District to enlist support for the CPP candidate. Realizing the political value of allying with the probably winning party, a large number of chiefs supported the CPP candidate, and in the general elections held that year he was sent to the Legislative Assembly with a clear majority of the votes.

Following the 1954 elections a clear polarization developed in the Tumu District between the CPP and the anti-CPP factions. Many of the literates, who felt disenfranchised by the CPP victory, allied with dissident chiefs and together they actively campaigned for the United Party (UP). In the 1956 parliamentary elections prior to Ghanaian independence, the UP candidate won by a narrow margin. On the national level, however, Nkrumah was gradually consolidating his power, and in 1960 the CPP was in unanimous control of the Ghana Parliament. In Nkrumah's attempts to rid himself of opposition the UP candidate lost his seat in Parliament on a constitutional technicality, and in 1959 the CPP candidate was returned to Parliament unopposed. From this point until the military coup in 1966 all political parties except the CPP were illegal, and with the final consolidation of the CPP the literates either directly joined or became affiliated with the CPP.

At the time of my fieldwork between 1966 and 1968 Ghana was being governed by a military council, the National Liberation Council or NLC, which had declared a moratorium on all political activity pending return to civilian rule.[1] Nonetheless, the Sisala's brief involvement in national politics had left its mark. The literates who at one time saw themselves as a united front stood divided among the various political factions. To many, "politics" came to be seen as an evil, bringing dissension and even causing families to divide against themselves. In terms of the traditional political system, conflicts which heretofore were held in abeyance by traditional authority and supernatural sanction not only came out into the open but also were given legitimate political expression. This involvement in politics has thus intensified those changes begun with the institution of chieftaincy, changes wherein the traditional values stressing unity and consensus are replaced by those of self interest, personal ambition, and ingratiation.

[1] Subsequent to my fieldwork, the NLC relinquished control of the country and in August 1969 the country returned to civilian rule with national elections.

5/The modern educational experience: the younger generation

For purposes of discussion, the "younger generation" is defined in the following pages as those individuals who have grown up under conditions of relatively rapid change and who have had early educational experiences at variance with those of the parental generation. While emphasis is placed upon the younger generation of Tumu, especially those who have been brought up in Tumu zongo, concern is also given to the villages, since with the establishment of schools and the increase in the number of returned migrants changes in the educational environment have also occurred there.

PARENTAL MEDIATION AND CHANGES IN THE CHILDHOOD ENVIRONMENT

In the preceding chapter it was explained how the experiences of the migrant and the early educated affected their adjustment to society and their relationships with fellow kinsmen. A further important aspect of this problem is the relationship of the acculturated parent to his children, for the acculturated parent inevitably affects changes in the traditional educational process.

When acculturated parents were asked to contrast their methods of child training with those of their parents, they often replied by referring to their experiences as migrants, noting that life in the South had taught them many lessons, including sense and self-reliance. The unacculturated Sisala, they say, is a good parent, but he is not able to teach his children about the ways of the modern world. The acculturated Sisala, on the other hand, has experienced this world and is aware of its dangers and pitfalls. One man explained his feelings as follows:

> We are living in a changing world and so we must teach our children about these things if they are not to suffer as we did. How your father raised you, you will raise your child in the same way. This is so that the child will not forget about the old things. But there are a few differences. [He points to his bicycle.] In our forefathers' time, if somebody wanted to borrow my bicycle, I would have given it to him. Today, people want money for those things. Also a short time ago, I was looking for a chicken to take to my

> in-laws. In our forefathers' time, the chicken would have been free. But now I had to buy it. All these things, I will teach my children. I will have to discuss with them that things are changing like this. These changes are good, because we cannot always remain in an uncivilized world. All of these things we are explaining here count in the civilized world. What you did once for free, you now do for money. There are many schools now. Our grandfathers didn't know about this. We are now in a civilized world.

This disposition on the part of the acculturated parent leads to a closer and more personal relationship between the father and his children. In the modified traditional setting of Tumu zongo those things which the father must teach the child are not necessarily inherent in his daily routine. If the parent is a wage worker, clerk, or teacher, the son does not accompany his father as the village child would follow his father to the farm. As a result, the process of home education has a greater element of conscious direction. The acculturated parent cannot assume that his son will grow up to take over the position of the father; rather he must inquire after his son's interests, discuss his problems with him, and help him acquire a position, whether it be farming, a trade, or schooling. This requires a greater degree of interaction and a greater concern with the particular interests and abilities of each child.

This greater personalization and informality has led to a breakdown of the authoritarian principles underlying the father-son relationship. As one man put it:

> This strict obedience, this is mostly on the part of illiterates. With educated people, if you tell your son something, he will have to speak his mind. If you find that the boy is right, you change your mind. With an illiterate, he just tells his son to do something. . . . In the old days, civilization was not so much. We obeyed our fathers whether right or wrong. If you didn't, they would beat you. We respected our fathers with fear. Now we have to talk with our sons when they challenge us.

Thus, the acculturated parent expects his children to demonstrate truthfulness and does not insist upon unquestioning obedience. In fact, it is often said that a child's inquiries, assuming they are not outrightly disrespectful, are necessary if he is to learn about the modern world. Parents also say that they would not punish a child if he was truthful and admitted to his misdeeds; instead, they would endeavor to explain to him why his actions were wrong and to make him admit his shortcomings.

The acculturated parent's concern in preparing his child to undertake a life in the modern world is demonstrated in his desire to educate his children formally. To a lesser degree this is also true for unacculturated Sisala, and among both the belief exists that formal education is the means by which success may be achieved in the modern world. The fact that a small body of Sisala educated elite was able to secure occupations of importance and prestige has served to create the impression that any child may be so educated and become equally successful. While the illiterate's perception of his social position is quite rigid, this attitude is not carried over to his children for whom mobility is seen as unlimited.

Significant differences are found, however, between the attitudes of the unacculturated illiterate and those of the acculturated illiterate with respect to formal education. Among the unacculturated villagers the original enthusiasm for establishing schools stemmed more from questions of intra-village rivalry and prestige than from the genuine desire to educate its younger generation. In many cases children were recruited by the village chief and elders for the express purpose of keeping the school open, since if school enrollment fell below a certain quota, the school would be closed by the Local Authority and this reflected upon the prestige of the village.

The unacculturated villager who sends his child to school regards education as an investment: a child who attends school will someday be able to earn good wages with which to help his father, or else attain an important position which reflects prestige on his family. School, however, is regarded as a luxury, and the parent seldom sends more than one, or at most two, of his children. The parent's main concern lies with the maintenance of the family homestead, and while the school boy is expected to obtain a livelihood other than through farming, he is nonetheless expected to serve his family and remain obedient to his elder's authority.

By contrast, the acculturated illiterate has a greater understanding of the educational process and a higher degree of personal involvement in the education of his children. In the preceding chapter it was shown that the acculturated illiterate develops through the migratory experience an acute awareness of his inferior position in the modern social hierarchy. This negative self-image, however, is opposed by the positive image he attaches to his educated children whom he views as superior to himself with respect to their eventual achievements. Thus, while he is limited by the real and believed incapabilities of his illiteracy, he can gain status and self-esteem by identifying with the achievements of his educated children.

The following statements give evidence of the father's negative image of himself as contrasted with the positive value attached to his children's schooling.

> Some parents feel they shouldn't send all of their children to school. But I have sent all of my children, since I have the strength to feed myself. Because when they pass out of school, the children will help me when I am weak. Also, when you don't send a child to school, you will want it to be just like you. For I don't know how to read and write, and I don't want my children to be like this. Now I have been asked to send my wife to the hospital. But if I did not have educated brothers, I wouldn't know whether the medicine they gave to me was good or bad. That is why a child should go to school. And in school, when the child passes out, he will be able to help the father out more. And if you are not sensible, you won't be able to do anything. A person who goes to school will be wiser and more sensible.

> School is important. In sending your child to school, you do it not only for business' sake, but also for civilization. One single educated person is worth more than we illiterates. These boys will become important men in Accra and overseas. We illiterates are never important. And in addition to the business side, such a person will be at the top of the illiterates. The educated person has a lot of privileges over the illiterates. Whenever he goes in company, he is seen over the illiterates. The educated person will be the head of the

> illiterates. A literate is more civilized than an illiterate. The literate can put something in writing that will last for 1000 years as a history for his grand, grand, grand, grandchildren to see. When an illiterate is dead, he is nothing.

The acculturated father's ego-involvement in the education of his children is reflected in the differential treatment given to school and nonschool children. While this is true to some extent in the villages, it is more common among acculturated parents living in the modernized setting of Tumu zongo. The school boy is frequently referred to as the "white man's child," and as such is usually not expected to participate in manual work or to learn the skills of farming or a trade. In fact, one father said that if his boy did badly in school, he would discipline him by threatening to make him go to the farm with his illiterate brothers. Many fathers, however, feel that they are incapable of properly disciplining their educated children, and they often relegate this discipline to the children's teachers, inquiring from the teachers about their sons' behavior and instructing them to discipline the boys accordingly.

This differential treatment is also seen in the methods used for positive incentive or reward. A nonschool child is not rewarded or praised for behaving well or performing a given task properly; instead, these things are expected of him, and it is believed that praise will spoil the child. However, school children are frequently given rewards in the form of praise or gifts for performing well in school. Most parents are aware of these differences, and thus the gifts are usually given secretly in order to avoid jealousy among brothers.

The differential treatment given school and nonschool children is more pronounced for girls than for boys. Here it is the mother who is deeply concerned with her daughter's future success. She feels that an educated girl is more civilized because she learns in school how to emulate the educated and refined behavior of other educated women: further, an educated girl will probably marry an important man who will give respect and gifts to his mother-in-law. Thus, many mothers show preference for schoolgirls by treating them like "ladies," buying them fine clothes, and discouraging their participation in manual tasks about the house.

This same set of distinctions between school and nonschool children is not found within literate family households, since literates invariably educate all their children. An educated Sisala man, by virtue of his wealth and position, is further often obligated to support and educate children belonging to his illiterate brothers. Since the literate is employed in a clerical, teaching, or governmental position, his occupation does not involve manual labor; accordingly his children are not exposed to any form of manual work. If the literate is relatively wealthy and has his own farm, he usually employs temporary wage workers rather than demanding his children work on the farm. The child of the educated parent is expected to devote all his time to his schooling and to attain a position either equal to or superior to that of his father.

Many of the changes which have taken place in the parent-child relationship may be attributed to changes in the familial and larger social environment. As discussed in the preceding chapter, a strong tendency exists among acculturated Sisala to form nuclear family households which are economically semi-independent from their larger traditional households. In this setting greater emphasis is placed upon interactional bonds within the nuclear family, with a concommitant weakening of the child's relationship with the larger family. This is particularly true for the residents of Tumu zongo and especially those who come from other villages. Living apart from his natal village, the child often grows up without a very good knowledge of his family and its traditions.

The following statement, given by a non-native resident of Tumu zongo, illustrates this weakening of the child's relationship to his father's family.

> When my children were young, I used to tell them stories about my village and about our family traditions. But in Tumu there are not so many people from my village and my children never went to visit the family. Now my children are educated and they have no time to sit with their father. A Sisala father usually farms with his son. But with educated people, they don't farm. They run around town with other boys. Soon we will forget our history. The educated man has a different character from his father. So fathers will die and never tell their sons about the important traditions. My children don't sit and listen to me anymore. They don't want to know the real things my father told me. They have gone to school, and they are now book men. Boys who are educated run around with other boys rather than sitting and listening to their fathers.

The weakening of familial and kin relationships has resulted in a breakdown of traditional parental social control. In the Tumo zongo where unrelated families often share the same compound, the father is empowered to discipline only his own children, and thus, if his child gets into a fight with a stranger's child or if the stranger's child acts disrespectfully toward him, he is powerless to mete out punishment. If he did, he may well become involved in a quarrel with the child's father.

Sisala parents say that it is difficult to raise children in the Tumu zongo, for the town has many bad children and a parent must be extremely observant lest his children fall into bad company. Children are instructed not to play with strange children, and they are usually required to inform their parents about their whereabouts. This is especially true for girls whom the parents fear might become pregnant; many parents refuse to send their girls to school for precisely this reason. "Bad parents" are those who do not teach their children to be respectful to strangers and who allow them to run freely about town.

The familial and larger social environment of Tumu zongo lacks the more or less rigid authoritarian structure of the villages, thereby providing the child with a greater number of alternatives for choice and action. In the villages the child's social space is oriented in terms of his minor lineage settlement; even when he grows older, he does not wander about the village without good reason to do so. Parental discipline is absolute, and the requirements of the subsistence economy structure most of the child's time.

In Tumu zongo, on the other hand, by the time the child reaches six or seven years of age, he is completely mobile within a social space which has no dominant focal orientation. His relationships at home are characterized by a greater degree of informality and those relationships contracted outside the domestic setting are not necessarily bound by ties of kinship. Unfettered by the work requirements of the village boy, the child has a great deal of free time in which he learns about his social environment independently of paternal guidance.

THE SCHOOLROOM EXPERIENCE

The public school system of Ghana is centrally controlled by the Ministry of Education which determines educational policy and curriculum standards and helps support extracurricular educational projects; its directives are implemented by regional and district representatives. The revenue used to support the primary and middle schools is derived from the local authority government of the administrative districts, except for those which are missionary or privately supported. In the Tumu District the schools are directly supported by the Tumu Local Authority which in turn receives its directives from the educational district office in Wa.

Ghanaian schools are similar throughout the country with nationally standardized examinations administered in the sixth year of primary school and the fourth year of middle school respectively. Except for the infrequently taught courses on tribal vernacular and tradition, all teachers rigidly adhere to the course outlines in the standardized syllabi prepared by the Ministry of Education. The subjects are of the British academic tradition, including English, mathematics, geography, history, science, health and arts and crafts. In many areas, as in the Tumu middle schools, religious education is included, and representatives of the various Christian and Moslem denominations come daily to speak to the students before classes begin. Prior to Nkrumah's downfall in 1966 a course entitled "civics" was directed toward political indoctrination and polemic. While the vernacular is used in the first two years of primary school, classes are thereafter conducted in English.

During the late 1950s and early 1960s the popular response to school construction was enthusiastic, and by 1960 twenty primary schools had been built in the Tumu District with 12 percent of the school age children in attendance. While this represents a significant increase from the World War II period, school enrollment among the Sisala is considerably below the 40 percent Ghanaian national average.

The village primary school is constructed of mud and thatch and usually contains two rooms; the six classes meet both in and about the schoolhouse. The minimal educational requirement for primary school teachers is a middle school leaving certificate, although better trained personnel with teacher training college education are recruited when possible. The two middle schools in the district are located in Tumu, one a day school whose students are either natives of Tumu or reside in Tumu with relatives, and the other a boarding school which serves those children from the villages. The middle schools are reasonably well constructed; each is equipped with a separate room for each class, and their teachers have all graduated from teacher training colleges. The Kanton Teacher Training College, located on the outskirts of Tumu, is a state-supported institution with a relatively small (14 percent) proportion of Sisala students.

The classroom environment into which the Sisala child enters is characterized by a mood of rigidity and an almost total absence of spontaneity. A typical school day begins with a fifteen-minute period during which the students talk and play, often running and screaming, while the teacher, who is usually outside talking with his fellow teachers, pays no attention. At 8:30 one of the students rings a bell, and the children immediately take their seats and remove from their desks the materials needed for the first lesson. When the teacher enters the room, everyone falls silent. If the first lesson is English, the teacher begins by reading a passage in the students' readers. He then asks the students to read the section aloud, and if a child makes a mistake, he is told to sit down, after being corrected. Variations of the English lesson consist of having the students write down dictated sentences or spell selected words from a passage on the blackboard. Each lesson lasts exactly forty minutes, at the end of which a bell rings and the students immediately prepare for the next lesson.

Little emphasis is placed upon the content of what is taught; rather, the book is strictly adhered to, and the students are drilled by being asked the questions which appear at the end of each assignment. The absence of discussion is due partially to the poor training of the teachers, yet even in the middle schools where the educational standards for teachers are better, an unwillingness exists to discuss or explain the content of the lessons. All subjects except mathematics are lessons in literacy which teach the student to spell, speak, read, and write.

Interaction between the teacher and his students is characterized by an authoritarian rigidity. When the teacher enters the classroom, the students are expected to rise as a sign of respect. If the teacher needs anything done in the classroom, one of the students performs the task. During lessons the student is not expected to ask questions, but instead is supposed to give the "correct" answers to questions posed to him by the teacher. The students are less intent upon what the teacher is saying than they are upon the reading materials before them. When the teacher asks a question, most of the students hurriedly examine their books to find the correct answer and then raise their hands. The teacher calls on one of them, who rises, responds (with his eyes lowered), and then sits down. If the answer is wrong or does not make sense, the teacher corrects him and occasionally derides him for his stupidity. In the latter case the child remains standing with his eyes lowered until the teacher finishes and then sits down without making a response.

The authoritarian rigidity which characterizes the classroom learning process is due in large part to the assumed authoritarian role of the teacher which stifles the student's free expression and creativity. However, both student and teacher are part of a larger sociocultural system which reinforces these learning and interaction patterns.

In the antecedent and ongoing traditional educational milieu the child learns to unquestioningly accept the directives and knowledge imparted by authority figures. The "true knowledge" (*namaka*) is based upon the wisdom of age, and by extension, upon the wisdom inherent in ancestral custom. Thus in any discussion or legal argument, *namaka* (that is, proverbs) are often quoted to give authority and credibility to an individual's statement. Similarly, the white man's knowledge derived from books is accepted on the basis of authority, and frequently when literates talk among themselves, they quote facts learned in school as *namaka*.

Another factor which serves to explain this authoritarian rigidity pertains to the role played by older students in the child's education. When a student enrolls in primary school and again when he enters middle school, he is regarded as a neophyte by the senior students and is often given lowly tasks to perform. This is especially true in boarding schools in which the seniors are given partial responsibility in the maintenance of discipline. The older students also quiz the younger ones on their school subjects and often ridicule them if they are unable to answer properly. Thus, within, and especially outside of, the classroom the older student occupies a position similar to that of an older brother in the traditional context, and in this relationship the younger student is expected to submit to his elder's authority.

A final cause may be found in the examination orientation of the Ghanaian school system, affecting not only the manner in which academic subjects are presented but also the student's attitude toward the learning experience. Teachers and especially headmasters are concerned that their students do well on the national examinations since they feel that this reflects favorably on their own merit as teachers and on the prestige of the Sisala tribe as a whole. Emphasis is thus placed upon rigid adherence to class syllabi and reading materials, and students are told that their ability to achieve literacy and retain necessary facts is the key to their future success. Thus, much of this rigidity is self-imposed by the students, and education comes to be perceived more as a means than as an end in itself.

THE ASPIRATIONS AND SELF PERCEPTIONS OF THE YOUNGER EDUCATED

Thus, the significance of the school room experience lies not so much in the content of what is learned, but in the students' perception of education as a means to the attainment of future life goals. This is nowhere more evident than in a series of projective essays written by students on the subject, "My autobiography from now to the year 2000."

One of the dominant characteristics of these essays is the optimistic and indeed naive perception that an almost one to one correspondence exists between formal educational achievement and success in later life. Most essays began with a methodical outline of the students' educational plans, beginning with graduation from middle school and extending in most cases to university and post-graduate education. At each stage in his life the student's educational accomplishments are rewarded by the assumption of a prestigious position in the society. These aspirations are usually quite unrealistic and demonstrate little awareness of conditions in the modern world. Their essays frequently become heterogeneous mixtures of educational achievements, material acquisitions, and assumed roles. Thus, it is not uncommon for a student to plan to earn three university degrees; buy a radio, automobile, and three-story house; have a zinc roof put on his father's house; marry a white woman; travel and teach in England and America; and then retire to his village with his wife and children.

The following statement demonstrates the staccato style of the essays and the students' perception of a society which is essentially open and in which all things are possible through education.

> In 1967 I will go to form four [middle school]. From there I will take the college exam [that is, teacher training college] and I will go to college. After my college I will come to teach in the middle school which I like. About some years to come, I will try again to take an exam to anywhere else. I will go to the university. . . . I will be there till I leave the upper form and then I will be a doctor. I will treat those who are sick and suffering from anything which I can care for. . . . I will be a doctor for a long period. And if I like, I will have my certificate and go and be a lawyer. There I will judge cases and the guilty ones will always be charged and taken to prison. I will judge my cases honestly and not dishonestly. . . . From there I will go and be the principle of a college or secondary school. There I will not teach but will only work in the office. Also I will see that the school is in good condition. . . . From there I will go and have a car, and there I will be a big man either an education officer, the district administrator, or the regional administrative officer. There I will have my own car and always carry my wife along with me. From there I will go and be the president of Ghana. There I will be the big man of the country. Whatever I say will be done.

When the essay materials are compared with data derived from interviews, a discrepancy is perceived between the students' aspirations and their actual expectations. It is usually admitted that the essay responses represent ultimate desires; however, students insist that the realization of such desires is possible, and they frequently cite cases of Africans who have arisen from humble beginnings to become important men in the society. Thus, the student's view of his future is a result of both educational achievement and fate. If he succeeds in life, it is because he has been fortunate enough to pass his leaving and entrance examinations in the various institutions of higher learning; if he does not succeed, it is because fate meant that he should not continue his schooling. As one student aptly stated,

> You see big men. They drive in cars. Whether I succeed or not, I don't know. Maybe I will become the president of Ghana or maybe I will just be a teacher in the villages. Nobody knows. It is what God wills, and I will be happy with whatever I become.

A second characteristic theme in the essays is the relationship between the student's desire to escape his inferior status as a school boy and his need to attain a position of power and dominance over others. Students describe their present status as one of wretchedness and poverty. They complain about their dirty appearance, tattered clothes, and insufficient diet; they also recall times when they were bullied or ridiculed by teachers and older students, or publically humiliated because of their poverty. The expressed desire to achieve success is a reaction of this perceived state of wretchedness. In describing their future occupational roles, students invariably make reference to their interaction with subordinates. Thus to be a magistrate is to pass judgment on evil people, or to be a head master is to give orders to classroom teachers. In effect then, the schoolboy sees himself as escaping his "small boy" status through education, obtaining an occupation or position concommitant with his educational level, and exercising the powers and prerogatives of his status.

The following statements demonstrate the relationship between the student's awareness of his poverty and his desire to achieve:

> When I have finished my schooling, I will sit down and think of the time when I was in middle school. And when I think of how poor I was and how I suffered, I will laugh at myself. For now I will have left the university. I will be a very rich man, and I will be sending some of the money home to my family.

> And there were those people who laughed at me when I was poor. But someday they will see me driving in a fine car, and they will be sorry. Maybe too, they will also be poor; and when they see me, they will ask for money. But I was as poor as anything once and God helped, so I will help anyone as poor as I was.

Another aspect to the schoolboy's negative perception of himself involves his familial, village and ethnic identity. If a boy perceives himself as poor, it is largely because his own father is poor and unable to furnish him with suitable clothing and spending money. Many schoolchildren recalled incidents in which they suffered humiliation as a result of their parents' poverty; this is particularly true among students from the villages who feel shame in the presence of the more acculturated Tumu people. Among the older students in the teacher training college the self-image of poverty is related to ethnic affiliation as Sisala. In this multitribal setting, the Sisala students often remark that they are referred to as "primitive" or "bush" by the students from the more acculturated tribes of the South.

The strong motivation to achieve thus implies not only a desire to escape the submissive status of the small boy but also a desire to raise the status of one's family and tribe. This motivational disposition resulting from familial and ethnic status withdrawal is directly related to a third dominant theme in the essays: the desire to serve as an educator and benefactor to one's people.

Whether the schoolboy's aspirations are high or low, he sees his eventual role in life as one of serving his own people. Not unlike the migrant, the typical imagery presented by the schoolboy is that of a young man who has become successful, who has traveled around the world and gained prestige, and who returns home to his village as a "big man." He sees himself settling down and building a fine house for his father and his own family. If he is wealthy, he will hire laborers to maintain the farm so that he and his parents will not have to work. He will also be generous both to his village people and to strangers, and with his superior knowledge and financial resources, he will endeavor to improve the conditions of his village.

The following statements illustrate the imagery which students attach to themselves in their future roles as "big men" and benefactors of their communities. The first describes the schoolboy's desire to alleviate the impoverished conditions of his people.

> My village people are dying of thirst. There is no good well there. There is no educated person there yet. I am the only school child. And may God bless me to complete my school, college, and perhaps university with success. During the old regime our fathers were troubled by hunger. Had I been an important person at that time, I would have demanded food from the government.

The second illustrates the school boy's impression of himself upon returning to his village as a wealthy and successful man.

> I have in mind this day being a professor so that I will be able to help my country. . . . As a professor I will visit so many countries such as America, Britain, and Holland. In fact, it will be interesting for me and my wife. . . . When I return, my father will be proud seeing his child like this. Just imagine me having a wife and children in my car moving down the street of my village. And when the people are in need of anything, I will help them.

The final excerpt involves a student's eventual goal of achieving recognition for the services rendered his people.

> By the time I have attained my graduation certificate from the university, the government will be so happy that they may like to make me president of my beloved country. When I receive my salary, I will divide the money and give part to my father and my wife and my children. I will take some money to the government to give me some laborers to put up nice buildings so that my village will also be remembered. By that, the people will be proud of what I have done. People say the U. S. A. is a beautiful country. But when they see my village, they will say it is more beautiful. Through my hard studies, my name will rise forever for people to remember.

While the essay responses of Sisala students, as well as those of other northern tribes, show a strong element of discontinuity between the school boy's unrealistic aspirations and his strongly dependent relationships to family and kin, the responses of acculturated southern students present a more realistic appraisal of their future living situation. Southerners are very much aware of the limited possibilities of educational and occupational advancement, and their responses reflect a deeper understanding of the actual workings of the modern nation state. Most see themselves as teachers or civil servants and their eventual life style as that of small, economically independent families. While they recognize the need to maintain customary ties with family and kin, such relationships are not central to their life ambitions. In short, the responses of southern students reflect an accommodation to the acculturative process wherein the customary demands of tribal life are not in conflict with their personal ambitions. Among northerners on the other hand, greater disparity exists between the realities of the modern plural society and the students' naive perception of their future roles in that society.

This disparity is directly related to a fourth dominant characteristic of the essays: a high incidence of projected and expressed anxiety about the future. In most cases this consists of a generalized or vague fear of the future and of life outside the tribal area; both are seen as strange and somewhat dangerous. In some of the more imaginative essays frequent incidents of projected failure in later life occur. Thus one student sees himself working hard for a university degree, but his progress is interrupted by the tragic death of both parents. Subsequently, he turns to drink and also dies a tragic death, his great ambitions gone unrealized. In other essays anxiety is expressed in terms of an ominous apprehension about the destruction of mankind, but the student sees himself as being able to prevent destruction through the exercise of his powers.

In crosschecking essay responses with interviews a genuine feeling of insecurity and anxiety was detected in the students' perceptions of the world outside the tribal environment. Many students, especially those in the teacher training college, remarked that they felt very much alone, lacking real guidance or assistance from their parents. Some admitted that they did not enjoy going home during the holidays because no one in their villages understood what they were studying in school. Yet most of the students stated that they did not wish to leave their tribal areas, except perhaps for a few brief visits to the South. The South, they felt, was more competitive than the North, and they expressed strong doubts whether they could succeed in an environment which they saw as basically inhospitable. Both the essay and oral responses of northern students thus show a genuine ambivalence: on one hand, the students are strongly motivated to attain modern occupational success; on the other hand, they are held back both by fear of being exposed to the hardships and ethnic prejudice of the modern urban South and by the need to maintain dependent ties with the more understandable world of village and tribe.

The essay responses of Sisala students reflect their experiences within the home and schoolroom environments. The fact that they place high expectations upon formal education as the one means of achieving success is due in large part to parental expectations placed upon the schoolboy. The desire to escape the submissive status of the schoolboy and to achieve a position of dominance is related to the psychodynamics of sibling conflict and growth in the traditional setting and to the dominant-submissive relationships between older and younger students in the schoolroom setting. Unlike the Euro-American notion of success which emphasizes self-reliance and personal excellence, the Sisala perceives his own success as inseparable from that of family, village, and tribe. In his future role as a successful adult the schoolboy aspires to a position similar to that of a prestigious elder man, serving as the nurturant benefactor of his people and gaining personal recognition for his generosity and beneficent power.

6/Conflict and sociocultural change

THE DILEMMA OF THE YOUNG AND INTERGENERATIONAL CONFLICT

THE SCHOOL BOY'S PERCEPTION of the successful life is patterned primarily after the lives of the older generation of Sisala literates. This perception as a direct, if not automatic, function of education reflects the historical fact that members of the educated elite have risen to positions of prestige and power within the Tumu District. During the 1930s only a small number of Sisala were educated, but in the postwar period emphasis was placed upon education for the purpose of preparing a body of indigenous literates to assume control of first local and then national politics. This change of policy meant that a relatively small body of educated Sisala gained easy access to a large number of prestigious government positions. Even those with only middle school educations became headmasters of schools, district commissioners, and members of parliament.

By contrast, the conditions to which the younger generation of educated Sisala must adjust are more severe and frustrating, particularly in respect to educational mobility. Most of the middle school graduates apply for entrance into the teacher training colleges and secondary schools, but few are able to qualify. This is due not only to the nationwide competition but also to political patronage and corruption. Gifts or "dashes" to such politicians in return for favors rendered is an all-too-common occurrence which has created an attitude of cynicism among members of the younger generation. Even in those cases in which students do qualify, financial assistance is frequently a problem, for many parents either are unable to furnish the necessary funds, or because of their lack of understanding, feel that their children have had enough education and should return to help their families. All these factors serve to limit the possibilities for educational advancement.

Upon graduation from middle school the schoolboy soon discovers that except for pupil teaching in the primary schools, few occupational opportunities are open to him in the Tumu District. Clerical positions in the government offices provide some openings, but these are few in comparison to the increased number of middle school leavers. A large number of Sisala literates thus migrate to the South in search of jobs concommitant with their perceived status expectations, but once in the South they discover that the living conditions are more severe than those in the tribal area. Food and lodging are more expensive, and nonmanual occupations are harder to secure. In addition, the minimally literate Sisala is seen by the Southerner as merely another Northerner and thereby is compelled by the socioeconomic conditions of the city to accept an occupation and life style similar to that of his illiterate tribesmen.

The position of village "pupil teacher" is in definite contrast to the aspirations or even minimal expectations of the schoolboy, for the wage rate for a "pupil teacher" is 370 new cedis (about $370) a year, which is not much more than the rate for common labor (about $250). In order to augment their income teachers frequently establish their own small farms and hire wageworkers to do the manual labor. Few teachers are provided living quarters in the villages, and most take room and board in the various minor lineage settlements. Living thus, the teacher is expected to comply with the authoritarian directives of the host house owner. The pressures for compliance with the traditional authority affect other aspects of the teacher's behavior; he may be called before the village chief to report on his actions and those of his fellow teachers. Because of the relative isolation of many Sisala villages the teacher is usually unable to visit Tumu or the village of his parents except during infrequent school holidays.

The young man's reaction to his position as village teacher is characterized by feelings of frustration, resentment, and resignation. Many complain about the low wages and the oppressive isolation of the villages, and frequent resentment is expressed at being treated like "small boys" by the village elder men. The following statement was made by a village teacher in his middle twenties:

> I am just a small man. I teach and I have a small farm in X [the village in which he teaches]. Maybe someday if I am fortunate, I will buy a tractor and farm for money because there is no future in teaching. When I went to school, I was told that if I got good marks and studied hard, I would be somebody, somebody important. I even thought that I would go to America or England. I would still like to go, but I don't think of these things very often because it hurts too much. You see me here drinking and perhaps you think I don't have any sense. I don't know. I don't know why I drink. But I know in two days' time, I must go back and teach school. In X, I am alone; I am nobody.

Much of this frustration and resentment is directed at the educated elite or "big men" who occupy the important positions of power and prestige in Tumu District. Such feelings are caused largely by the failure of this elite group to meet the expectations of the educated younger generation. Many of the younger literates strongly believed while in school that they would grow up to serve their people and nation. National organizations such as the Young Pioneers and Boy Scouts, which placed stress upon citizenship and public service, helped to reinforce the image of Ghana as a progressive and democratic nation state. It was in this context that members of the younger generation saw their teachers and other important Sisala literates—not only as models upon whom their lives would be patterned but also as sources of advice and aid in the pursuit of their eventual goals. The educated elite were seen as most able to understand their problems in contrast to their nonliterate parents and in many cases students took up residence with literate kinsmen rather than remaining in their parental households. Thus, a gradual transfer of identification took place from the nurturant and protective image of the nonliterate and often unacculturated parent to the expected nurturant and protective image of the educated Sisala "big man."

In response to the perceived resentment and criticism of the younger generation, the older Sisala literates defend their position by criticizing the younger generation for being lazy, apathetic, and having had an easier life. They proudly point out that they had to walk seventy miles to school in Lawra and that they thus learned the value of education and hard work. The younger literates are seen as weak in character and as desiring success without working for it, and cases of drunkeness and irresponsibility are frequently cited for the reinforcement of this image.

The following statement was made by one of the older literates:

> Some people feel that education is better today than before but I don't agree. Written work was better then. The teachers of today were my students. They can't work sums and their English is poor. The material today is more complex; there are better syllabi; but the teachers don't work as hard. When they have free time, they drink and are lazy rather than spending their time constructively. When they teach, they just sit in their chairs and don't move around when they talk. Often the secondary level teacher teaches over the student's head. They feel that they are superior to the head teacher and won't take his advice. In the old days, we would prepare our lessons and use pictorial aids. Now everything is prepared for the teacher, and he doesn't have to do any work at all. . . . In the old days there was competition among the teachers. Today if one teacher does poorly, he will connive with others to bring the standards down. The young men are not competitive or constructively competitive. Now they try to tear down the successful young man. They don't make up or compete. They will just call the successful young man by the term "kundo" or "big man" and will shun him. The same is true with both students and teachers. In the old days when a child did poorly and they announced his grades, he was very much ashamed. But today, children who fall below the mark just laugh.

Statements on both sides contain elements of truth, and these truths reflect some of the deeper social problems confronting not only the Sisala but a large part of Ghana as well. It is true, for example, that many of the younger Sisala literates, reacting to disappointment and frustration, have become apathetic, turned to drink, or in other ways lost faith in their ability to succeed. It is also true that the educated elite practice the politics of self-interest and patronage; however, this is not considered a serious fault, since most members of the younger generation readily admit that in a similar position they would also be concerned with their own welfare and that of their family and kin. The most significant truth is the fact that since

Ghanaian independence an increase in the number of primary and middle school leavers has occurred in the Tumu District while educational and occupational opportunities have remained static. The "big men" have not been able to deliver the scholarships or in other ways fulfill the promises which the younger generation of literates has perceived them as having made.

One effect of this situation has been a polarization between the generations and a loss of respect on the part of the younger generation for the elder generation. This is reflected in the often derogatory terms *kundo* or "big man" and *kolo* or "colonial man," used by the younger generation to refer to their literate seniors. Student descriptions of the term *kolo* in a sentence completion test include: doesn't know anything, is too proud and boasts too much, talks without sense, makes false promises, is not all that civilized, causes wars, is afraid of the white man, wears baggy trousers, and knows nothing about football. In contrast to this negative imagery, the younger generation of literates sees itself as more attuned to the times and to the current styles of dress, music, and language, and less dependent upon the white man and "colonial mentality" than the older literate generation.

Schoolboys march in a parade celebrating the first anniversary of Ghana's military government.

In contrast to the young educated, the young acculturated illiterate does not visualize himself as part of the struggle for success and prestige. His expectations are low-keyed and realistic, and he sees his life largely in terms of a trade in which he is now engaged or which he hopes to acquire. Work is considered as rewarding in itself, and most of the young acculturated illiterates are very industrious individuals. One young man interviewed had spent five years in the city of Tamale to learn a trade. The first two years were spent as an usher in a movie theater and half his salary was placed in the bank while he lived in impoverished conditions on the other half. When he had saved enough money, he apprenticed himself to a master tailor. Upon becoming a journeyman, he did manual labor for another two years in order to save enough money to buy a sewing machine and cloth. Such cases of industriousness and dogged pursuit of goals are not common among the younger literates.

These attitudes of hard work and initiative may be attributed in large part to the differential upbringing and training of the illiterate. Most parents, whether acculturated or unacculturated, admit that they raise their illiterate and literate sons differently. While the discipline and training of the school boy is left largely to his teachers, that of the illiterate remains in the hands of his father or fathers. He is expected to do farm work and no allowance is made for the fact that his literate brother does not have to engage in manual labor. The illiterate son is usually closer to his father than his educated brother, and if his father is an artisan, he often works closely with him and thereby learns a trade.

Since the literates represent a minority of the Sisala population, it might be argued that the effects of intergenerational conflict are limited. In some respects this is true, since many literates do make successful adjustments, settling down as village teachers, offering their wages to their fathers, accepting the marital arrangements of their families, and serving their families as wage earners. However, with the growth of education and increased outmigration from the Tumu District, a very real cycle of conflict between generations has emerged. This problem is most intense in Tumu, especially within literate or acculturated families.

We have seen that the schoolboy or "white man's child" has been brought up to believe that someday he will be a wealthy and prestigious "big man" in his society. This self-image has been created and reinforced both by parental training which stresses the differential and favored treatment of schoolboys and by the schoolroom experience and the child's identification with his teachers and other prestigious Sisala literates. Upon graduation the schoolboy is confronted by a world which is frustrating to his ambitions, and so he comes to resent those literate "big men" with whom he had so strongly identified and who have subsequently disappointed him.

One reaction to this frustration has been a desire to avoid being shamed by having others perceive his lowly image of himself. While the young literate may privately admit to his condition, he would never project this image to others of his acquaintance, especially his own family. He therefore goes to considerable lengths to maintain a prestigious life style, buying fine clothing, expensive shoes, and expensive cigarettes and drink. This life style is maintained on a relatively meager income and often in the absence of any income at all. The literate son, assuming that he is working, is frequently unable to offer his wages to his father, and in fact, he may be deeply in debt to his landlord, friends, local creditors, and proprietors of the local beer bars. He frequently contracts large debts in order to pay off other debts, and this cycle places strains on his relationships and may lead to public humiliation and shame when he is not able to meet his debts. This shame and humiliation also involves the literate's family which frequently has to dispose of some of its property in order to pay these debts.

In recent years there has been a reaction on the part of parents toward the behavior of the young literates, most often expressed in terms of disillusionment. When asked to comment on education, many parents merely shake their heads, saying that they had thought that their sons and daughters would have learned "civilization" and returned to help their elder people. They feel that education has made their children lazy and "useless," that their children are too proud to help their fathers on the farm, that they have become careless and reckless with their lives, and that they often disgrace their family's name.

Disillusionment also characterizes a more general criticism of the whole ongoing process of change. While the villagers have relatively little contact and involvement with modern politics, they are nonetheless aware of the corruption, patronage, and especially the unfulfilled promises of politicians. Further the schoolhouse and the presence of young schoolteachers represents a concrete manifestation of the modernization process, and frequently the image of the village teacher is a negative one. The villagers complain that the teachers do not show respect for the village elders or bother to inform them of day-to-day happenings in the school. They also accuse the teachers of being remiss in their duties and of exploiting students by making them work on their farms.

Many parents have begun to refuse to send their children to school, or to withdraw those children already in school. Statistics from the Tumu Local Authority show a gradual decrease in primary school enrollment over the past five years and this decrease is especially evident in the lower forms of primary school. In many villages it is not uncommon to see a teacher without any students in his class. While this decrease in enrollment represents a reaction to the entire institution of modern education, it is usually triggered by a specific conflict or grievance between the teachers and the traditional authority. The following incident, related to me by the headmaster of a primary school, is a case in point.

> One day Mr. X made a trip to Y [a village outside Tumu]. He parked his car on the road and was away for some time. When he returned, he saw that somebody had defaced his car, beaten it with sticks or something. Now I knew that my school children knew something about this. So I gathered them together and told them that if they were good citizens, they should report to me who did it and God would reward them. So I found out that this was done by some people in the village. When the village people found

out that their children had told me such things, they were very angry. They said that the teachers were teaching their children to disrespect their elders. It is because of things like that that the fathers are taking their children out of school.

The extended family is also able to exercise considerable control over the literate's life. Since all Sisala are dependent upon family and kin and since dependency is both psychological and economic, the thought of severing one's ties and leading an independent life would only represent an act of extreme desperation or reaction to shame. This dependency allows the family to place pressures upon the literate's behavior. If, as is frequently the case, the young literate becomes disrespectful and refuses to help his family economically, his family may react by refusing to provide assistance for necessary customary obligations. This is especially true in marriage, since the literate is unable to make the transactions by himself. If he is employed and earning wages, his family may require him to contribute his wages to meet a customary obligation which would normally have been paid for by the family as a whole. These pressures often become stronger when members of the literate's generation succeed to the position of authority within the family. The incidence of conflict and sibling rivalry becomes stronger at this time, and the young literate no longer enjoys the favored treatment he received when his fathers were alive. Many schoolboys, when speaking of their educational aspirations, say that if their fathers died, they would not be able to continue their education because their brothers would not help them.

The economic pressures placed upon the literate by his family and kin only increase the frustrations already felt as a result of restrictions upon his educational and occupational advancement. On one hand, the young literate who has been raised to expect success is unable to accept failure. To return to the farm and engage in manual labor not only would be difficult because of lack of training but would also mean a loss of face, a negation of the literate's self image. In addition, the fact that he has failed in his altruistic expectations of being a benefactor to his people affects the very legitimacy of his self image as a purposeful and useful member of society. On the other hand, the literate's family and kin also shared these high expectations for success, although their expectations included the notions of filial piety and family loyalty. The failure of the literate and his disrespect for parental authority are seen as resulting not from the social conditions which limit educational and occupational mobility, but from the failure of modern education and from the weaknesses in the schoolboy's character. The young literate is thus lazy, useless, and in need of discipline. The confrontation of generations becomes an impasse, and parental pressures, rather than resolving the problem, only add to it.

This schism between generations has led to the breakdown of norms governing the legitimacy of age and seniority in Sisala society. This is seen most clearly in the high incidence of alcoholism among members of the elder generations. Prior to 1945 the production and sale of alcoholic spirits, as opposed to native beer, were outlawed in northern Ghana as a result of British policy which sought to keep the North free from the "corrupt" influences of the South. After 1945 when the ban was lifted, distillers from the South came North and began brewing a rather strong alcoholic spirit called "apoteshe." The price of apoteshe was very high, and its consumption represented a sign of wealth. Many old men who became addicted sold family property in order to purchase it, and many who were wealthy subsequently became poor. This frequently caused deep family divisions, and many young men left home in disgust at their fathers' behavior and poverty. While the price of apoteshe has since decreased, its consumption has nonetheless increased.

This high incidence of alcoholic consumption is directly related to the anomic and demoralized state of many members of the elder generation. When asked why so many elder men drink, one man explained:

> One problem is that a man may have a lot of people in the house, but all of them are in the South. So you get old and cannot take care of your people. In our Sisala way, a man with a large family is rich. But an old man will sit down after the harvest, and he will see his friends bring in big harvests while his is small, and he wonders why God has done this. So he will drink and try to forget. For example, X [an elder man] used to have many brothers in the house. Then they died or went South and so did his sons. So he has many worries and does not know why he should live.

To many of the older generation old age has become a period of sadness and despair; growing old means to become poor and lonely. The traditional blessings of old age—large family and propertied wealth—do not materialize and the old men worry that the household they have strived to nurture and protect will die upon their deaths. Drinking is a response to despair, and it is not surprising to note that one of the nicknames given to apoteshe is "kill me quick."

The increase of drinking behavior on the part of the Sisala, both young and old, has served to accelerate the already existing tensions between generations through the breakdown of mutual respect. An elderly man who turns to drink loses the respect inherent in his role as benefactor and protector of his family. This loss of respect, as well as the literate's perception of his father's poverty, is in itself a further cause of despair and alcoholic consumption.

A young man who drinks heavily is frequently referred to as "careless," meaning that he "cares less" about living and only desires to drink and live life very quickly. While such a person disregards the normal conventions of respect and decorum, he nonetheless cares very much that he should never appear poor and wretched. Even a "careless man" must dress well, have friends, and have money for drink in order to maintain an image of wealth and generosity. The drinking behavior of both the older and younger generations thus represents a reaction to the frustration of unattained goals, and the loss of respect caused by this deviance further serves to widen the gap between the generations.

"POLITICS" AND CHANGE: PROPERTY, AUTHORITY, AND THE SUPERNATURAL

When asked to describe the current state of human affairs, the Sisala frequently quote the proverb, "Today's people" (*jining nia*). Though its meaning is vague and indefinite, the proverb represents a negative valuation or criticism of the direction of change in terms of its effect upon people's character and their conduct in social relationships. When asked to explain the meaning of this proverb, one man stated:

> Nowadays, people are not cooperating. They always wait to see your downfall before they laugh at you. They talk good of you when you have something to give them. But once you are poor and have nothing to give them, they will retreat from you and talk bad of you.

In the words of another:

> In the old days, there were real friendships. People cared about one another and they were generous. Today each man is caring only about himself. The big man exploits the poor man, and the poor man waits for the big man to fall and then he laughs. We no longer respect people, we exploit them. Everything has become politics.

It is difficult to determine the antiquity of this proverb. Whether in fact it has always existed as a criticism of the divisive potentialities of Sisala society is not known, but it does reflect the current times, the rise of self interest, and the decline of the traditional values defining human conduct and societal order.

The pursuit of self-interest is reflected in the ongoing breakdown of the extended family unit. In Chapter 5 it was shown that acculturated illiterates and literates tend to establish household units apart from those of the extended family, and the child raised in this limited familial context attaches primary loyalty to his real father and frequently knows little about his family and lineage traditions. In educating his children the acculturated father is concerned that they become successful so that they will help him in his old age, but this concern is usually selfish because the father is motivated more in terms of his own self-interest and prestige than in terms of that of his family and kin.

The placing of primacy on the real father-real son bond is a negation of the important moral principle which gives brothers reciprocal rights in each other's children. If the young literate chooses to give nothing to his father's brother, he is by custom committing an act of gross disrespect to his father's brothers, to whom he should at least make a customary offering. When a literate becomes successful and his biological father becomes noticeably wealthier than his brothers, deep resentment, jealousy, and conflict often result.

The tendency toward the formation of smaller familial units is directly related to the growing distinction between "personal" and "family" property.

Traditionally almost all property was owned collectively by the family, and inheritance passed collaterally to the next elder member of the household. The splitting of family property was a violation of ancestral custom; even former articles of personal property such as clothing, tools, weapons, and medicines took on a ritual significance upon the death of the owner, and if not destroyed, became part of family property. With the advent of wage-work and monetary income, it became possible to hold property independently of the family. Articles such as bicycles, automobiles, and bank accounts constitute forms of property which are not subject by custom to family ownership. Monetary wealth is by nature liquid and more easily disposed of than traditional objects of wealth such as cattle, farmland, and houses. Wealthier literates frequently speak of dividing up their money among their children during their lifetime, and most of those who invest in their children's educations see this as a form of life insurance for their later lives.

Rights in private property are frequently the subject of conflict, since no definite rules exist governing the extended family's or house owner's rights in the personal wealth of one of its acculturated members. While the acculturated person is expected to offer his wages to his family head, this is regarded as a "kindness" or act of mutual respect and is not specifically prescribed by ancestral custom. Thus the acculturated person may occupy a position of economic advantage, for while he is not required to help his family, his family head is obliged to help him in the performance of his customary obligations or face loss of family prestige. Thus, if a delinquent member of a family refuses to contribute to the purchase of a goat to be given at his in-law's funeral, the family head must supply the offering or incur the disrespect of the in-law's family.

The conflict over the rights of the extended family in the personal wealth of one of its members becomes acute at the time of inheritance. By custom the head of the extended family has claim to the property of one of its deceased members. This he holds in the name of the family, controlling it for the collective good of the *janwuo*. However, with the increased tendency toward economic independence and the ownership of private property, a man may wish to leave his belongings to his wife and children, especially in the case of migrants who live apart from their extended families and whose children feel but minimal allegiance to their kin. This very factor of spatial distance serves to weaken the larger family's control and in the event of the man's death, patrimony usually passes to his wife and children without the knowledge of the extended family. In addition, a man's last will and testament is regarded as inviolable by Ghanaian law; thus any claim which might be made by the extended family on the basis of tradition would not stand up in a court of law.

This issue has not yet become a common reality, since most acculturated members have not yet reached their elder years; however, in cases where it has occurred, the resultant conflicts often lead to permanent schisms in intrafamilial relations. The refusal to submit to the tradition of offering one's father's wealth to the head of the father's family constitutes a serious blow to the prestige of the *diatina* who is expected to be able to control and affect unity within the larger family. Such an action diminishes not only his power but also the strength of the *janwuo* as a whole. Since the transmission of property is directly related to mortuary custom and ritual, this refusal also affects the very religious structure upon which familial continuity is based. If a man dies and is buried outside the tribal area, his extended family still performs certain necessary funeral rites so as to insure the dead man's place in the world of the ancestors. In the event of inheritance conflict these rites are often not performed, especially since it is necessary for the eldest son of the deceased to be present at their performance. Thus the consequences are severe; for while the son may inherit from his dead father, he is in the larger sense both economically and ritually disinherited from his patrilineal kinsmen.

We have thus far examined the process of conflict and change in the context of intrafamilial relationships and institutional changes in property and inheritance occuring within the family. These changes represent a breakdown of the traditional values affirming sibling unity and filial piety, values which are directly related to intravillage amity, the legitimacy of authority, and man's relationship to the supernatural. Changes occurring at the family level thus have a cumulative effect, in turn affecting more far-reaching changes in the larger politicoreligious institutions which define the social order.

It has been shown that the introduction of the institution of chieftaincy meant the beginning of far-reaching changes in the norms of Sisala social organization. Authority had stemmed from the age and inherent "wisdom" of the village elders and *jangtina* (village owner) whose duties were to affect consensus and repair conflict; supernatural power and justice were perceived as serving these needs. The chief's authority, although initially derived from British support, gradually came to be based upon personal wealth and the possession of charismatic or personal magical powers. While the chief may profess to serve the interests of the entire village, the nature of his position as a secular authority serves instead to promote and perpetuate his own interests and those of his immediate family and kin. The methods of bribery, patronage, and ingratiation which have come to be associated with modern politicians are inherent in the institution of chieftaincy. Unlike the *jangtina* the chief may and often does act without the expressed consensus of his village elders. The advent of modern political involvement during the late 1940s added a new dimension to the role of the chief, for modern literate politicians frequently made deals with the chiefs which entailed giving a "dash" (monetary favor) and making political promises. The result is that the playing of "politics" involves not only politicians but also chiefs who see their futures and fortunes related to the ongoing process of change in the modern nation state.

The cumulative effect of these related phenomena has been a breakdown in the values supporting the legitimacy of authority. As one man stated:

> In the old days, a chief was elected by his elder men, and he served his people. Today, chiefs no longer consult their elder men. They talk with politicians. They are wanting only money. For example, the chief of A was wanting to rent a lorry to take him to the House of Chiefs in Bolgatanga, but his elder men gave him no help. So he had to rent it with his own money. . . . With politicians, they aren't concerned with the small man. In CPP times, a minister or some other big man would come to Tumu. You would invite him to your house and he would see that you have some fine things—some glasses or utensils. And so he would ask to see them, and you would never see them again. He would take them. With a "big man," all he has to do is convince the chiefs and he is elected. And once he is elected, there is nothing you can do. We give these people fear, but we don't respect them. We have a proverb: Poor man, no friends. You see, when a big man is powerful, everybody gives him respect because they fear him. But when he falls, they laugh.

The big man or ambitious chief, though retaining the respect which connotes "fear," does not possess *zile* or respect emanating from goodness and generosity and he is no longer seen as being able to provide and care for his people.

While the potential for divisiveness has always existed in Sisala society, its actualization was always controlled by the belief in the supernatural efficacy of the ancestors and other spiritual shrines. With the breakdown of the norms defining authority and moral conduct, a parallel breakdown has occurred in the beliefs concerning the efficacy of supernatural means of social control.

This fact is reflected in the recent historical decline in oath taking and in the greater tendency to resort to court action in the settlement of civil disputes. Disputes among members of a village were traditionally settled by an informal hearing before the village elders, and if the case were serious or irreparable by informal consensus, the village shrine was considered the final and absolute arbitrator. Until about 1955 the village shrine of Tumu, the Tumuwihiye, was regarded as the most efficacious of all shrines in the Tumu District, and most civil disputes involving traditional matters were brought before it. In those days, the Sisala say, a man told the truth or else he knew that he would die, but today such civil cases are brought before the magistrate's court in Tumu. Swearing oaths in court is farcical; I have many times observed Moslems swearing on the Bible and Christians on the Koran. As a consequence, no sanction is in force against lying, and the court cases become involved and frustrating as the magistrate attempts to reconcile sharply contradictory statements.

To bring a civil dispute before the magistrate's court is viewed as a disgrace both for the litigants and their families and village people. A civil case often exposes details of the litigants' family lives which are regarded as private matters, and since the magistrate court sessions are always well attended, these matters become the subject of public gossip. Such disputes also reflect badly upon the village as a whole and the village chief in particular. The Sisala frequently comment that these particular disputes should have been settled in the village. The fact that an intravillage dispute is brought to court demonstrates that the village chief is unable to affect unity and achieve consensus among the component lineages, and the same holds true of the subdivisional chief in intervillage disputes.

Throughout the Sisala tribe there is a growing awareness of the general state of anomie and the breakdown of supernatural sanctions and established authority. The two following statements represent typical explanations for this breakdown. The first statement, by a literate Christian (Baptist), views this breakdown as a good development resulting from civilization, though civilization is also viewed as being responsible for what is bad.

> In the old days, a man could not argue with his compound head because the spirits were on his side. If a man insulted his father, his father would curse him and he would die. The spirits would come and kill the son, just like that. But today, there is civilization, and all of the fetishes are losing their power. The witches are not so much now. Today nothing happens to a young man who does these things. Once there was a boy in town who was a teacher, who beat up his father in front of a lot of people and nothing happened to him. In the old days, he would have died the next day—the spirits would have got him. Civilization is good, but you can't beat your father. Even if your father is wrong you must not disagree with him. I would never let my son do such a thing to me, or I would sack him from my house. With civilization you respect your father. The Christian faith gives you this respect.

The second statement, given by a literate native resident of Tumu, also demonstrates a strong relationship between civilization and the breakdown of traditional supernatural sanctions. In this case, however, civilization in the form of modern religion and missionaries is viewed as evil.

> Modern religion is bad. It has caused people to lose their decency and respect. The Baptists and the Catholics tell you that you will be punished after you die, so it makes no difference what you do now. In the Sisala way, if a person did bad, the gods would punish him right now. In the old days I would put some money down and nobody would steal it because they feared being struck by lightning. In the old days, if money were found, it would be given to the *jangtina*. He would then buy an animal and sacrifice it to the fetish, and the meat would be shared among all the people of the village. Today, nobody cares. A young man would steal money even if it were lying on the fetish.

These statements point up a close, if not one-to-one, relationship between the moral conduct of the human community and the belief in the efficacy of the ancestors and other spiritual shrines. Civilization, perceived for the most part as a blessing, is also seen as the cause of moral decline. The fact that political corruption and infractions of ancestral custom are allowed to exist unpunished by supernatural retribution threatens the credibility of beliefs in the forces which are supposed to maintain the social order. This breakdown is most evident in Tumu where the anomic influences of change have been most intense, but a similar lack of respect for the efficacy and justice of village shrines is evident in villages where intravillage conflict exists and respect for authority is declining.

7/Toward a new synthesis: Sisala Youth Union and Sisala Literate Association

During the Christmas holidays of December 1967 and January 1968 two organizations were formed in the Tumu District—the Sisala Youth Union (SYU) and Sisala Literate Association (SLA). These associations represent the first deliberate and organized attempts to repair the perceived state of hostility and disunity among the Sisala of the Tumu District.

The Christmas holiday is a time when many Sisala come to Tumu to celebrate and to renew old friendships. These include not only the teachers in the villages but also Sisala living in other parts of Ghana. One such person was a student at the University College of Cape Coast and the founder of the Sisala Youth Union.

The following is a copy of a statement he prepared, announcing the proposed aims of the Union, in which membership is reserved for both literates and illiterates under the age of 30 years.

> Dear brother/sister,
>
> Formation of "Sisala Youth Union" (S.Y.U.)
>
> It has become very necessary that a Sisala Youth Union be formed within the Tumu District. You will without doubt agree with me that there has remained no modern tradition left by our great grand brothers and sisters for us to follow. We may not call this a failure on their part, but a mere lack of initiative. Whereas almost every District around us has formed an organization or a union, we have never dreamt of one. We can therefore justify our initiative, now or never, in our mother land by planting a permanent and durable tradition for our youth to show to the outside world, that, after all, we are also capable of forming a more pronounced Union.
>
> Below are the proposed aims of the Union:
>
> 1. To foster brotherhood in the Sisala District and to encourage the social integration of the Sisala Youth. To establish a very firm pattern of tradition.
> 2. To help the younger generation who is coming up to achieve fruitful goals. This can only be done by inciting and motivating them to let them improve their aptitude in all their undertakings such as education, farming, trading, etc.
> 3. The Union will form a curriculum which will guide the Sisala youth to have respect for the elders [father, mother, sister, and brother]. As we all know the indigenous Sisala have gained credit for their world wide respect, honesty and culture. We must come out now to revive it. For

example, the Sisala District came out with flying colors in dancing and certain sporting activities some decades ago but suddenly collapsed to its bed. It is not the fault of the youth but the society which corrupts and sets in jealousy and unscrupulous acts among the youth.

4. It will be an attempt to bring together our runaway brothers (outside Tumu) to meet in Tumu at least once a year. In such a gathering, efforts will be made to portray the recognition of the district. Publicity of the district is completely nil whereas other areas of less population than Tumu have news agencies.
5. The Union will also resolve ways and means of solving the problems of our brothers who sometimes fall into conflicting difficulties such as finance, choosing of careers, and marriage problems, etc.
6. The aim of the Union is not a deliberate attempt to segregate. It is not another apartheid in Africa but an organization whose achievements will be beneficial to the country as a whole.
7. Membership will be restricted to only Sisala by birth whose ages are not more than 30 years. In due course the age group may well be defined to suit the meaning of the word "youth," but in the meantime, all who fall into this group are welcomed.

The first meeting or get together to draw up the constitution will be on the 29th December 1967, at the Tumu Community Centre. A constitution will be drawn and officers elected. Officers will include the President, the Vice-President, the Secretary, and his assistant, the Treasurer.

Note. The above proposals are subject to criticism of any nature by anybody, provided it is not going to poison the formation of the Union.

The meeting was held as scheduled, and it was attended both by literates and illiterates, all under the ages of thirty. The presiding officer, however, was one of the oldest literates of Tumu who began the proceedings by announcing that he was there simply to preside and that the young people should do all the talking. His speech, like all those which followed, was given in Sisala. The organizer of the SYU next commented that most of the people in attendance were literates, and he hoped that this group would eventually form the nucleus for a larger group. He felt that many of the young men were afraid to come without their elder men being present. He continued by saying that the Sisala people had been disgraced and that young people must work and fight for themselves and their culture. He read through the mimeographed sheet he had distributed, but when he reached the proposal concerning age qualifications for membership, he became slightly embarrassed and said that this might have to be changed. He said that the union should not be separated from the elder people of the town, although he felt that the young people could speak better and more honestly as a group among themselves.

After his talk several young people gave short speeches stressing the importance of unity as a precondition to individual and group accomplishments. Proverbs were quoted, all revolving around the theme of unity. Following the speeches officers were nominated and elected and the meeting was adjourned.

Three days after the meeting of the Sisala Youth Union, the Sisala Literate Association had its first meeting, quite possibly in reaction to the formation of the Sisala Youth Union, since most of the people in attendance belonged to the older generation of literates. Unlike the SYU, the Sisala Literate Association had a literacy requirement, and the mood of the meeting, which was conducted in English, reflected the genuinely elitist character of the association.

Much of the meeting was taken up by speeches, stressing the themes of unity and the need to repair previous conflicts through collective action.

> We must erase self interest. For if we are to be a strong district, we must be unified. Self interest must only exist within the state. It must be controlled by the police.
>
> Self interest is real. It is natural to man and to deny this is to be dishonest. What is more important is to have honesty in our relations. We must not hold our grievances inside ourselves. We must air our grievances to each other so that we can repair them.
>
> We are evolving. Now we are in the year 1968. We must know our place in history. Politics came to Tumu in 1954 and caused us to separate. We must now be unified. This group here can be the light of the district. And if we don't stand as literates, the whole district will fall. For now the devil is raising its ugly head [i.e., rumor and suspicion].
>
> I am more bent on tolerance and forgiveness. Most important, we must listen to what people have to say. The illiterates often spread political rumors. Yet we must listen to these, even if we reject them. My wife and I are a society. If there is a quarrel, I must be able to understand and forgive or else the society will split.
>
> We must be able to forgive. If I get into a quarrel, I will try to find someone elderly to settle it. For thirteen years, we have not been able to meet and discuss things freely like this.
>
> This gathering is the starting point to bring unity. Certain things went wrong in the district. We have not been friendly and tolerant to each other. We have been back biting. Now we must come together and fight in the interest of the district.

During these speeches one of the older literates introduced the question of the Sisala Youth Union saying that there was a rumor in town that the SYU plans to rule and depose all the older big men. He suggested that the SYU be disbanded, since it would only create conflict. The organizer of the SYU, who attended the meeting, replied as follows:

> The purpose of forming a youth union was to embarrass the older people so that they would also form a union. Those literates belonging to the young union will also be members of the literate association. We shall always respect and be a part of the mother union. [He then read the mimeographed list of proposals.] Point seven [that is, that part pertaining to age qualifications] is wrong, and in the future the group will include people up to the age of 45 years.

Some debate occurred, but it was finally agreed that the Sisala Youth Union should be allowed to exist, since as one man said, "their juvenile ideas" would not hurt anything.

The remainder of the meeting was concerned with naming the association and appointing a platform or constitutional committee. Four people, all younger members of the older generation of literates were nominated and elected. The older literates, many of whom had held positions of importance in the former CPP government, declined to participate. Some debate occurred over whether the association should include illiterates and the idea was rejected, since most members felt that the literates could act as spokesmen for their illiterate brothers.

The constantly expressed theme of unity stems from an awareness that the Sisala tribe and the Tumu District have in recent years fallen into bad repute as a result of politics, backbiting, and jealousy. In part, this emphasis represents a revival of traditional values stressing mutual respect and unity through consensus or "being of one mouth." However, the SYU and SLA are also manifestations of an evolving synthesis based upon the realities and problems of the modern world and upon the emergent lines of stratification in Sisala society. This is clearly seen in the differing ideologies of the two associations.

As its name indicates, the Sisala Youth Union is oriented to the problems of the "under-thirty generation." It makes no distinction between literates and illiterates, though the literates have obviously assumed the positions of authority. Neither is a distinction made between the Sisala of the Tumu District and those living elsewhere in Ghana. As a tribal union its aim is to bring back the "runaway brothers" by building a cultural tradition of which the younger generation can be proud. The Sisala Youth Union is thus concerned with rebuilding the younger generation's faith in its society and affecting unity through mutual aid and self help.

Among the older literates of the Sisala Literate Association the problems of conflict and factionalism are more serious. Most of these people were formerly involved in politics, incurring many hostilities among themselves in the process. The meeting of the SLA thus served the additional function of catharsis. While stressing the importance of unity, great emphasis was given to the causes of interpersonal animosity. The problems of jealousy, self-interest, "rumormongering," and backbiting were all discussed, and although no one actually confessed to past misdeeds, each obviously recognized his own faults and those of others. The fact that this group of literates was able to come together and discuss its common faults was in itself a move toward unity and away from the dissensions that had previously split villages and families.

Nonetheless, the Sisala Literate Association still possesses a strong political element, as clearly seen in the debate concerning the legitimacy of the Sisala Youth Union. In contrast to the SYU, the members of the SLA see themselves as the natural leaders of their people, and the fact that the association excludes illiterates and conducts its meetings in English reflects this elitist attitude. The SYU, while neither elitist nor primarily political, does represent a genuine innovation in terms of Sisala society. In the traditional society no formal age sets and societies are present, and affiliations and loyalties are defined solely in terms of family, village, and kin. In this setting seniority is the prime determinant of interaction, and little independence from one's elders' authority is possible. The formation of the Sisala Youth Union is thus a genuine cultural innovation developing in response to the disillusionment and alienation of the younger generation. As an innovation it is also perceived as a threat to the established authority. The rumor that the young people were going to usurp the authority of their elders represents more a projection on the part of the older generation than the reality of the SYU. When the organizer of the SYU appeared before the SLA meeting, the members who challenged him were those whose authority stemmed solely from seniority. These were individuals of minimal education who had acquired positions of importance during CPP times, but who were now unemployed. The organizer of the SYU, who is far better educated than almost all the older literates, is better qualified to hold a position of importance and power and therefore constitutes a threat to the status of his elders.

Seen in the larger perspective, the Sisala Youth Union and Sisala Literate Association are significant manifestations of the transitional state of Sisala society wherein the traditional values defining man's position and conduct are being increasingly modified by those of the modern social system. Traditionally a man's position was defined in terms of affiliation to kin; family, lineage, and village provided the anchors for the individual's identity, and the worship of the ancestors embodied the final moral-religious justification for human existence. While these values are still operative, the modern world has made its inroads. Migration, wage work, formal education, and participation in politics are experiences foreign to the traditional system and as previously seen, have led to the painful erosion of the traditional values of Sisala society.

In contrast to these ongoing conditions of anomie and social disorganization, we are also witnessing the gradual development of a new synthesis of status groupings, based in large part upon the commonality of educational experiences and upon similarities in socioeconomic position. Notwithstanding the large percentage of Sisala living in terms of the traditional life style and subsistence economy, three such groupings may be found in the society. The first is that of the acculturated illiterates and former migrants living in small household units and engaged as wage workers, artisans, and petty entrepreneurs. Their common educational experience is that of migration and life in the city; and the formation of extrakin and extratribal relationships, along with affiliation to Islam, constitutes the manifestation of their new identity. Next there is the older educated elite united by age, education, status, and a sense of mission which finds expression both in political participation and in the formation of the Sisala Literate Association. Lastly there are those of younger generation, albeit mostly the literates and students, who were raised in the changing times of high expectation and who have come to know disillusionment and alienation.

To regard these groupings as social classes, however, would be a misconception, since none of them is mutually exclusive of the others and since individuals usually occupy roles in more than one social category. At the same time these groupings are real insofar as the individual utilizes them as points of reference on which to anchor his identity. The formation of the Sisala Youth Union and Sisala Literate Association, therefore, demonstrates a formal recognition or consciousness of these new identities, and the very existence of these organizations constitutes a historical precedent, clearly signaling the future trends in Sisala culture change.

Glossary

SISALA TERMS

bahiang: "eldest son," referring to the eldest male of the junior generation within the extended family
banihiang: elder man
bayila: man song (sung at the funeral of an elder man)
bichuola: useless child
dalusun: medicine
dalusuntina: "medicine owner" or medicine man
diatina: "house owner" or head of the extended family
dima: the human soul
fa: to fear; to respect with fear
hachikuoro: woman doctor and midwife
hila: witch; male witch
jang: village
jangtina: "village owner" or village headman
janwuo: patrilocal extended family, referring to both the family and the compound with it inhabits
jaraang: bride price paid by the family of the groom to the family of the bride
jechiking: minor lineage settlement
kiatina: "owner of things" or wealthy man
kuoro: chief; wealthy man
mallma: elder sibling of the same sex (also includes the older children of one's father's brothers and mother's sisters.)
nadongngo: friend
namaka: proverb, historical legend, or any statement of moral truth
nang: mother (also refers to one's mother's sisters, mother's co-wives, and father's brother's wives)
ngana: younger sibling of the same sex (also includes the younger children of one's father's brothers and mother's sisters)
nyimma: father (also refers to one's father's brothers and by extention to any patrilineally related male of the first ascending generation)
-tina: a suffix denoting ownership
tintein: the earth; a section of land; female high god
tome: a class of personal spirits relating to hunting (*tome*), divining (*vuruga tome*), blacksmithing (*lukuru tome*), xylophone playing (*luri tome*), and praise singing (*goka tome*)
vene: shrine and the spiritual deity inhabiting the shrine
venetina: "shrine owner" or one who cares for and sacrifices to a particular shrine
-viara: suffix denoting clan or patriclan
vuruga: diviner
wijima: "knowing things," referring to sense, knowledge, and wisdom
zile: mutual respect or respect accruing from goodness and generosity

ANTHROPOLOGICAL TERMS

ACCULTURATION: the process of culture change in which one society often occupying a subordinate position, is greatly influenced by another

AFFINAL: pertaining to kinship ties through marriage

CLAN: an exogamous kinship group whose members are related to one another through ties of patrilineal descent to a remote and oftentimes legendary ancestor

CLAN SECTION: that segment of a clan which inhabits a particular area or village

COMPOUND: an approximately circular structure, consisting of several dwellings, which houses the members of the extended family.

DIVINER: a religious practitioner knowledgeable in the supernatural art of foreseeing future events and discovering hidden knowledge

EXOGAMY: the custom of marrying outside one's social group; Sisala clans are exogamous

EXTENDED FAMILY: a domestic group consisting of more than one nuclear family unit

LINEAGE: an exogamous kinship group, of lesser magnitude than a clan, whose members are related to one another through ties of patrilineal descent to a common known ancestor.

MATRILINEAL: pertaining to descent traced through the female line

PATRILINEAL: pertaining to descent traced through the male line

PATRILOCAL: pertaining to the custom whereby a married couple establishes residence with the husband's family

POLOGYNY: the marriage of a man to two or more women at the same time

SORAL POLYGYNY: a polygynous union in which the wives are sisters

ZONGO: a generalized West African term pertaining to a migrant or nonindigenous settlement within a larger town or city

References

ALLPORT, G. W., and J. W. GILLESPIE, 1955, *Youth's Outlook on the Future.* New York: Doubleday & Company, Inc.

ERIKSON, E. H., 1963, *Childhood and Society.* New York: W. W. Norton & Company, Inc.

EYRE-SMITH, S. J., 1933, *A Brief Review of the History and Social Organization of the Peoples of the Northern Territories of the Gold Coast.* Accra, Ghana: Government Printer.

GHANA CENSUS OFFICE, 1962, *1960 Population Census of Ghana: Volume II, Statistics of Localities and Enumeration Areas.* Accra, Ghana: Census Office.

———, 1964, *1960 Population Census of Ghana: Special Report "E," Tribes in Ghana.* Accra, Ghana: Census Office.

GOLD COAST CENSUS OFFICE, 1932, *The Gold Coast, 1931.* Accra, Ghana: Government Printer.

———, 1950, *The Gold Coast: Census of Population 1948.* London: Crown's Agents.

HAGEN, E. E., 1962, *On the Theory of Social Change.* Homewood, Ill.: The Dorsey Press, Inc.

BARRY, H., M. K. BACON, and I. L. CHILD, 1957, "A Cross-Cultural Survey of Some Sex Differences in Socialization," *Journal of Abnormal and Social Psychology* 55:327–332.

BARRY, H., I. L. CHILD, and M. K. BACON, 1959, "Relation of Child Training to Subsistence Economy," *American Anthropologist* 61:51–63.

LANDY, D., 1959, *Tropical Childhood.* Chapel Hill: The University of North Carolina Press.

MCCLELLAND, D. C., 1961, *The Achieving Society.* Princeton, N. J.: D. Van Nostrand Co., Inc.

———, and G. A. FRIEDMAN, 1952, "A Cross-Cultural Study of the Relationship Between Child Training Practices and Achievement Motivation Appearing in Folktales," *Readings in Social Psychology,* G. E. Swanson, T. M. Newcomb, and E. H. Hartley, eds., New York: Holt, Rinehart and Winston, Inc.

WHITING, J. W., I. L. CHILD, and W. LAMBERT, 1966, *Field Guide to the Study of Socialization.* New York: John Wiley & Sons, Inc.

Recommended Reading

Apter, D., 1966, *Ghana in Transition*. New York: Atheneum Publishers.
A general account of the political development of Ghana from colonial times through independence.

Doob, L. W., 1960, *Becoming More Civilized.* New Haven, Conn.: Yale University Press.
A crosscultural study of the sociopsychological reactions to colonialism and Westernization in Africa, Jamaica, and among the American Indians.

Fortes, M., 1938, *Social and Psychological Aspects of Education in Taleland.* London: Oxford University Press.
A study of the traditional process of cultural transmission in a northern Ghanaian tribe.

Foster, P., 1965, *Education and Social Change in Ghana.* Chicago: University of Chicago Press.
Contains a general account of the history of formal education in Ghana with special emphasis placed upon its relationship to the process of change.

Henry, J., 1960, "A Cross-Cultural Outline of Education," *Current Anthropology* 1:267–305.
A good methodological guide to the issues and problems involved in a cross-cultural study of education.

Herskovits, M. J., 1967, *The Human Factor in Changing Africa.* New York: Vintage Books.
A sensitively written study on the broad subject of changing Africa. Chapter 8 deals specifically with education.

Kaye, B., 1962, *Bringing Up Children in Ghana.* London: George Allen & Unwin Ltd.
A general survey of traditional child-training practices among selected tribes in Ghana.

LeVine, R. A., 1966, *Dreams and Deeds: Achievement Motivation in Nigeria.* Chicago: University of Chicago Press.
An interesting study of the relationship between achievement motivation and traditional tribal background.

Manoukian, M., 1952, *Tribes of the Northern Territories of the Gold Coast.* London: International African Institute.
A systematic description of the customs and beliefs of the tribal societies of northern Ghana. Contains an excellent bibliography.

Rattray, R. S., 1932, *The Tribes of the Ashanti Hinterland.* Oxford, England: Clarendon Press.
An ethnographic survey of the tribal societies of northern Ghana. Chapters 51 through 55 deal with the Sisala.

Spindler, G. D., ed., 1963, *Education and Culture, Anthropological Approaches.* New York: Holt, Rinehart and Winston, Inc.
A collection of articles dealing with education in America and by comparison with the educational process in other areas of the world.